HOW TO PLAY METAL GUITAR

THE BASICS & BEYOND

EDITED BY RICHARD JOHNSTON

Backbeat
Books

San Francisco

Published by Backbeat Books
600 Harrison Street, San Francisco, CA 94107
www.backbeatbooks.com
email: books@musicplayer.com

An imprint of the Music Player Network
Publishers of *Guitar Player, Bass Player, Keyboard,* and other magazines
United Entertainment Media, Inc.
A CMP Information company

CMP
United Business Media

Distributed to the book trade in the US and Canada by
Publishers Group West, 1700 Fourth Street, Berkeley, CA 94710

Distributed to the music trade in the US and Canada by
Hal Leonard Publishing, P.O. Box 13819, Milwaukee, WI 53213

Text and cover design by Richard Leeds — bigwigdesign.com
Front cover photo by Jay Blakesberg
Back cover photo by Jude Gold

ISBN 0-87930-775-7

Printed in the United States of America
04 05 06 07 08   5 4 3 2 1

CONTENTS

INTRODUCTION

Heavy metal. Speed metal. Death metal. Rap metal. Industrial metal. Nu metal. From the time it began in the '60s—when the likes of Pete Townshend and Jimmy Page shoved rock guitar front and center with crunching riffs and crushing volume—metal has spawned dozens of spinoff styles, all the while remaining rock music's most powerful force. Poised defiantly on rock's far fringe, metal is the beast of rock guitar—devouring the meanest sounds music has to offer and spitting out the rest.

Even as it has bred myriad mutant offspring, "traditional" metal guitar has refused to die—it remains the foundation for today's many metal manifestations. That's why you aspiring metal monsters have much to learn from masters like Page, Ritchie Blackmore, and Eddie Van Halen. They laid the groundwork for the guitarists who emerged when metal collided with styles like grunge and funk in bands such as Alice in Chains and the Red Hot Chili Peppers, and they've provided the inspiration for the heavy-metal torchbearers in bands such as Metallica and Megadeth as well as for the current crop of 7-stringers and dropped-tuners in groups like Korn and Coal Chamber.

We've gathered lessons from all of those players, and more, in *How To Play Metal Guitar*, as presented by the expert teachers of *Guitar Player* magazine. In addition, to assist you in your quest for heavy tone we've garnered indispensable advice on gear and recording from dozens of great players and producers, and to guide your ears through the work of metal masters past and present we've included a discography of essential recordings. And speaking of ears, our friends at TrueFire.com have laid down the licks for you to hear at an exclusive *How To Play Metal Guitar* Web page—check page 9 for details. As always, thanks are due Brad Wendkos and the gang at TrueFire for their tireless help putting together the online lessons. Thanks also to Andy Ellis for his suggestions for the book's content, to Amy Miller for helping pull it all together, and especially to the writers of *Guitar Player* and to the players whose music *GP* illuminates year after year.

One more note on ears: Death metal may be cool, but deaf metal is definitely not. The folks at HEAR—Hearing Education and Awareness for Rockers—have all the latest information on hearing protection waiting for you at hearnet.com. Listen up!

—*Richard Johnston, Editor*

ABOUT THE AUTHORS

Andy Ellis is editor in chief of *Frets* magazine and a senior editor of *Guitar Player*. In addition to his performing and studio credits, Andy originated the Sessions instructional series.

Joe Gore is a *Guitar Player* contributing editor whose performing, producing, and engineering credits include work with such artists as Tom Waits, PJ Harvey, Bijou Phillips, the Eels, and Stella Soleil.

Jude Gold is a *Guitar Player* associate editor who has gigged and recorded with artists such as George Clinton, Stu Hamm, and Eddie Money.

Jesse Gress is the author of Backbeat's *The Guitar Cookbook* and *Guitar Lick Factory*. Jesse tours and records with Todd Rundgren and the Tony Levin Band, and he has served as music editor on several Backbeat titles.

James Rotondi is a former *Guitar Player* features editor whose performing credits include gigs with the Grassy Knoll, Mr. Bungle, and Jettatura.

Dave Whitehill, best known as Roy Buchanan's teacher and Steve Vai's transcriber, has written dozens of song folios, magazine articles, and transcriptions.

NOTATIONAL SYMBOLS

The following symbols are used in *How To Play Metal Guitar* to notate fingerings, techniques, and effects commonly used in guitar music. Certain symbols are found in either the tablature or the standard notation only, not both. For clarity, consult both systems.

4● : Left-hand fingering is designated by small Arabic numerals near note heads (1=first finger, 2=middle finger, 3=third finger, 4=little finger, t=thumb).

p● : Right-hand fingering designated by letters (p=thumb, i=first finger, m=middle finger, a=third finger, c=little finger).

②● : A circled number (1–6) indicates the string on which a note is to be played.

⊓ : Pick downstroke.

∨ : Pick upstroke.

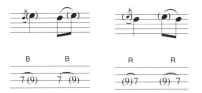

Bend: Play the first note and bend to the pitch of the equivalent fret position shown in parentheses.

Reverse Bend: Pre-bend the note to the specified pitch/fret position shown in parentheses. Play, then release to indicated pitch/fret.

Hammer-on: From lower to higher note(s). Individual notes may also be hammered.

Pull-off: From higher to lower note(s).

Slide: Play first note and slide up or down to the next pitch. If the notes are tied, pick only the first. If no tie is present, pick both.

A slide symbol before or after a single note indicates a slide to or from an undetermined pitch.

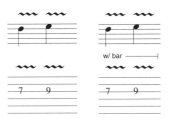

Finger vibrato.   Bar vibrato.

Bar dips, dives, and bends: Numerals and fractions indicate distance of bar bends in half-steps.

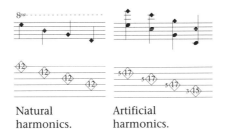

Natural harmonics.

Artificial harmonics.

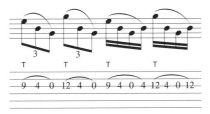

Pick-hand tapping: Notes are hammered with a pick-hand finger, usually followed by additional hammer-ons and pull-offs.

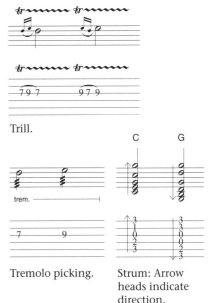

Trill.

Tremolo picking.

Strum: Arrow heads indicate direction.

HOW TABLATURE WORKS

The horizontal lines represent the guitar's strings, the top line standing for the high *E*. The numbers designate the frets to be played. For instance, a 2 positioned on the first line would mean play the 2nd fret on the first string (0 indicates an open string). Time values are indicated on the standard notation staff seen directly above the tablature. Special symbols and instructions appear between the standard and tablature staves.

CHORD DIAGRAMS

In all chord diagrams, vertical lines represent the strings, and horizontal lines represent the frets. The following symbols are used:

━━━━━ Nut; indicates first position.

X   Muted string, or string not played.

○   Open string.

⌒   Barre (partial or full).

●   Placement of left-hand fingers.

||| Roman numerals indicate the fret at which a chord is located.

Arabic numerals indicate left-hand fingering.

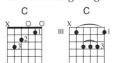

HOW TO PLAY METAL GUITAR

FREE AUDIO LESSONS

All of the lessons featured in HOW TO PLAY METAL GUITAR are available online, in audio MP3 format, for immediate download AT NO EXTRA COST. Now you can hear how the lesson examples are supposed to sound when played by the pros. Get your free audio lessons now and start learning the basics and beyond!

How to Get Your Earful

1) Go to PlayMetal.TrueFire.com.
2) Register the Backbeat code printed on the inside back cover of this book.
3) Download lessons to your desktop.

$10 Bonus From TrueFire!

If you're new to TrueFire, after registering and downloading your lessons, you will be e-mailed a TrueFire Cash certificate good for $10 worth of additional lessons on TrueFire. Choose from over 1,200 killer guitar lessons written and performed by top artists and instructors.

POWER CHORD PRIMER

A Lesson in Loudness

BY DAVE WHITEHILL

You probably won't find the term "power chord" in a music dictionary, even though this forceful harmonic entity has been the foundation for billions of rock riffs over the past decades. Actually, what most guitarists refer to as power chords are really harmonic intervals known as perfect 5ths, but there are other varieties. Though containing only two notes (standard chords contain three or more), 5ths are treated like chords in rock music and, like all chords, are represented by letter names.

For example, the first chord in Ex. 1 is called *A5*; it consists of an *A* (the root note) and *E* (the 5th note of the scale). Play Ex. 1 in its entirety and you'll have the *A* minor scale (or Aeolian mode) harmonized in 5ths. Except for the diminished (or flat) 5 on beat *two* of bar 1, all these intervals are perfect 5ths.

When we harmonize the *A* major scale in the same fashion, as in Ex. 2, a diminished 5th occurs on the 7th degree. Don't get too bent out of shape by this academic explanation—power chords are really just any group of notes that sound ballsy with distortion—though it can't hurt to have some harmonic know-how behind your barrage.

Ex. 1

A5 B(♭5) C5 D5 E5 F5 G5 A5

Ex. 2

A5 B5 C♯5 D5 E5 F♯5 G♯(♭5) A5

You now have the raw materials for your own power chord riffs in the key of *A*. You can transpose these chords to other positions on the fretboard and even experiment with harmonizing other scales in 5ths, such as the *A* Dorian (*A–B–C–D–E–F♯–G*), *A* blues scale (*A–C–D–D♯–E–G*) and *A* Mixolydian (*A–B–C♯–D–E–F♯–G*). The following riffs should give you an idea of some of the possibilities available to you. The examples are short, reflecting the repetitive nature of a lot of power chord songs. Don't be afraid to repeat them over and over. Try different tempos, but once you start playing a riff, keep the tempo consistent. A good metalhead keeps things solid rhythmically—it's half the challenge.

Example 3 is a variation on the ever-popular I-♭VII-♭VI progression featured in songs like Dokken's "Breaking the Chains," Hendrix's "All Along the Watchtower," Aerosmith's "Dream On," and Led Zeppelin's "Stairway to Heaven."

A fairly standard heavy rock crunch pattern, Ex. 4 introduces some syncopation for more movement. First concentrate on sounding tight, keeping noise between chords to a minimum by muting slightly on the bridge with the outside of your palm. Then let your right hand float free and really slam into the chords—let the noise rule! Try this one at a medium tempo first, and then play around with different tempos.

Ex. 3

A5 G5 F5 G5

Ex. 4

A5 C5 D5 F5 E5 C5 D5

Example 5 features an *A* major riff reminiscent of the melodic punk sound of the Ramones and other power pop bands. Again, try cycling this riff over and over, muting slightly for a controlled sound on two or four repetitions, and then for the next four, letting the chords ring out for that wall-of-guitar sound. Or tighten up on the *A5* and *E5* eighth-notes and strum hard, and open while sliding those passing chords (*D5–F♯5* and *C♯5–B5*). Remember, even in the simplest riffs the dynamic possibilities are endless. This one sounds best played fast and hard.

A funky ditty based on the *A* Mixolydian mode, the medium-tempo passage in Ex. 6 works well with some finger vibrato on the chords; try shaking the second *G5* and the *D5* a bit before releasing them.

Ex. 5   **Ex. 6**

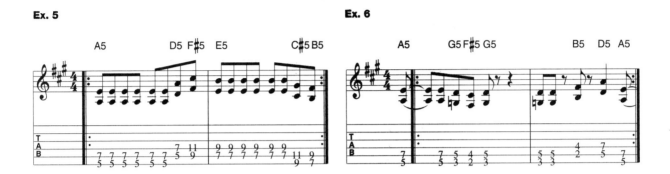

The *A* Dorian mode is the source of Ex. 7, a rhythm pattern in the style of early Kiss. Try really laying into those power chords on the "and" of beat *four*, letting them ring, then striking just as hard on beat *two*, but only letting it last for a short eighth-note. Wearing black-and-white makeup and skyscraper-heeled boots may help you with this one.

Example 8 opens with a fuller-sounding *A5* and *G5* than in the previous examples, due to the fact that the roots for both are doubled. The harmonized scale used here is *A* blues. The distinctive ♭5 (*E♭* in this example) of the blues scale has endeared it to metal and thrash bands like Black Sabbath, Metallica, and Testament. In like style, you may want to try muting bar 2's chords (resting the side of your picking-hand palm lightly against the bridge) for that throaty metal sound. Downstrokes rule here.

Ex. 7   **Ex. 8**

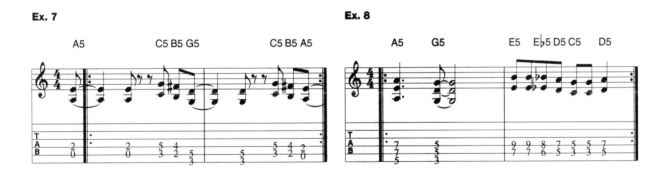

When you invert a perfect 5th and place the root on top, the result is a perfect 4th. The *A* blues scale phrase in Ex. 9 combines both 5ths and 4ths, and recalls Ritchie Blackmore's signature stomp riffs from Deep Purple and Rainbow. In the example, *G–C*, *A–D*, and *E♭–B♭* are all perfect 4ths.)

In Ex. 10 both intervals are again combined, but this time there are some hammered-on 4th chords. The lick in bar 2 is based on a rather exotic scale: the 5th mode of the *D* augmented Gypsy scale (*D–E–F–G♯–A–B♭–C♯*). Exotic scales gained popularity from their use in progressive thrash bands like Megadeth.

Ex. 9

Ex. 10

Ex. 11

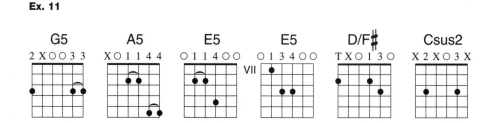

Additional note doubling in conjunction with open positions gives perfect 5ths the big, clanging sound associated with bands like AC/DC. Ex. 11 shows chord diagrams for some of the most commonly used open power chords. The first one, *G5*, requires you to mute the 5th string with the 2nd finger of your fretting hand. The root is tripled and the 5th is doubled in this voicing, as in the *A5* that follows. Check out the differences in character of these two forms of *E5*. The next two chords are not based on perfect 5ths, but are still members of the power chord family. The first inversion of a *D* major chord (*D–F#–A*), *D/F#* is often used as a passing chord going to *G5*, as in the central riff to AC/DC's "Highway to Hell." Featuring stacked 5ths, the form of *Csus2* shown here is a great substitute for a regular *C5*.

Some of the best rock rhythm riffs are loosely based on an idea called "pedal point," a compositional device that involves playing a series of chords over a sustained bass note. On guitar, pedal point gives the illusion of a bassist and guitarist playing together, even when the chords and bass notes aren't played simultaneously. Pedal point–type riffs like the one in Ex. 12 are great for intros featuring a solo guitar—check out Ted Nugent's "Cat Scratch Fever," Deep Purple's "Burn," and Ozzy Osbourne's "I Don't Know." Mute the bass notes with the heel of your picking hand in all examples to enhance the effect of the guitar/bass illusion. Examples 12–16 are in the key of *A minor*, using the *A* string as the pedal tone, but an *E*-string pedal is popular, too, particularly in the speed-metal music of Metallica and Megadeth. So try moving these patterns down one string as well.

The chromatic progression in Ex. 13 demonstrates that a major 3rd (the last interval in the progression) can work as a power chord. Example 14 uses the *A* minor scale harmonized in 3rds to give this pretty power riff a sound similar to some of Def Leppard's chordal work, while Ex.15 shows how melodic movement can be incorporated into power chord patterns. Pedal point and power chords are combined in Ex. 16 on a funky riff based around *A* Mixolydian and an *A7* (*A–C#–E–G*).

Ex. 12

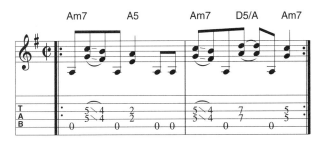

Ex. 13

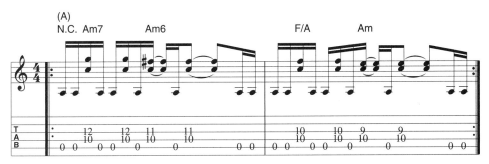

Ex. 14

Ex. 15

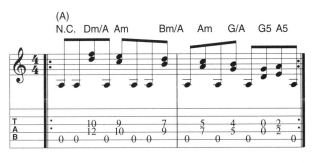 

Though it appears to depart from the key of *A*, Ex. 17 is based on the *E* Phrygian dominant mode (*E–F–G♯–A–B–C–D*), the fifth mode of the *A* harmonic minor scale (*A–B–C–D–E–F–G♯*),. It works well with Ex. 15, especially as a turnaround.

Examples 18 and 19 are played in dropped-*D* tuning, which you can achieve by tuning your 6th string down a whole-step to *D*. The lowered pitch gives an extra subsonic crunch preferred by bands from Slayer to Soundgarden, before bands such as System of a Down and Korn began exploring even lower tunings and extended low sounds of the 7-string guitar. (See the lesson that starts on page 17). In our last two examples the partial barre is all that's needed to play grungy perfect 5ths on the 6th and 5th strings.

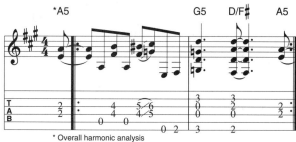

*A5   G5   D/F♯   A5

* Overall harmonic analysis

Ex.17

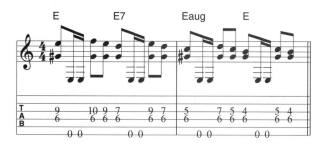

E   E7   Eaug   E

Ex. 18

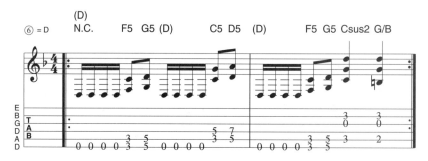

(D) N.C.   F5 G5 (D)   C5 D5 (D)   F5 G5 Csus2 G/B

⑥ = D

Ex. 19

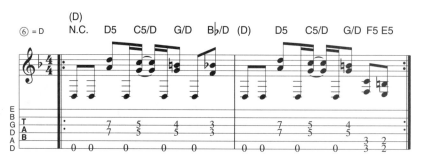

(D) N.C.   D5   C5/D   G/D   B♭/D (D)   D5   C5/D   G/D F5 E5

⑥ = D

    The examples in this lesson are variations of riffs you've probably heard. For further inspiration, listen to songs by your favorite power-chord purveyors. When you're ready to write your own, sit down with a tape recorder and let your creativity take flight. If you have trouble improvising at first, start with a basic concept—like the pedal point. After you get some parts on tape, you can start arranging them into songs. Try linking riffs that work together melodically. Don't be afraid to try different keys—modulations add variety and drama to your compositions. And don't forget: The first word in "power chord" is power. Let it rip!

A CRASH COURSE IN 7-STRING GUITAR

Shake, Rattle & Rumble with These Low-tuned Riffs and Grooves

BY ANDY ELLIS

Today's rockers have embraced the 7-string guitar with such enthusiasm that one could easily assume it's a hip, new invention. In fact, the 7-string has been with us for centuries.

During the 1800s, Russian classical-guitar virtuosos plucked 7-string instruments. (You can hear this stirring music on *The Golden Age of the Russian Guitar* [Dorian Recordings] by 7-string master Oleg Timofeyev.)

In the 1940s, fingerstyle wizard George Van Eps drew complex jazz harmonies from his archtop 7-string, calling it a "lap piano." But it took Steve Vai—with his tsunamic tone and astounding chops—to reveal the 7-string's potential to '80s shredders and launch the modern movement. With the likes of Orgy, Korn, and Limp Bizkit relying on the 7-string for their rumbling riffs, deep-toned guitar has finally become a mainstream instrument. Not long ago, the 7-string was a custom ax. Today, most guitar manufacturers offer at least one model, and you can buy nice 7-strings for under $1,000.

Like its 6-string sibling, the 7-string guitar can be tuned in various ways. In 19th-century Russia, *DGBDGBD* (low to high) was the accepted standard. This is like combining open-*G* guitar tuning with Dobro "high-*G*" tuning. Van Eps tuned his 7-string *AEADGBE*.

Today, the most common 7-string tuning is *BEADGBE* (Ex. 1). Notice how strings 6–1 are identical to regular guitar. Dipping five ledger lines below the staff, the bottom (7th) string corresponds to low *B* (3rd string, 2nd fret) of a 4-string bass—that's *deep*. (See Fig. 1 for a comparison of the ranges of 7-string guitar, 6-string guitar, and 4-string bass.)

Ex. 1

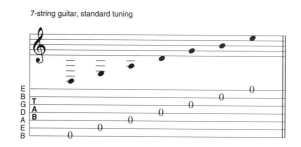

Fig. 1

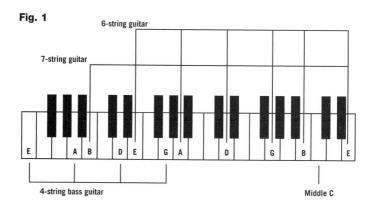

Let's limber up with a moody passage inspired by System of a Down's "Spider." The band's guitarist, Daron Malakian, tunes his 6-string Ibanez Iceman to *CGCFAD*—that's dropped-*D* tuning lowered a half-step. (He strings the Ibanez with Ernie Ball .011–.056 sets.) His clangy riff adapts nicely to 7-string, as shown in Ex. 2. The low-*B* pedal-tone (open 7th string) adds a rich drone below the 5th string's graceful melody. The trick is to pluck the low *B* softly so it doesn't overwhelm the melody. Go for a clean, clangy tone and watch the accents—they define the rhythm. This example's string-skipping structure will challenge your picking-hand technique.

Ex. 2

Ex. 2 cont.

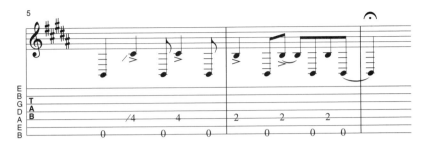

Also offering string skips, Ex. 3 pays homage to Limp Bizkit and the band's 7-string-wielding Wes Borland. Distilled from "My Generation," this riff combines "disco" octave jumps with some mean palm muting—'70s funk bass collides with Dick Dale. In each measure, notice the staccato marks (beat *one*) and the sneaky grace-note hammers (beat *three*). To generate those low, staccato C♯s, simply release your 1st finger halfway through beat *one*. Hammering into *E* from open *B* gives you a nanosecond to leap from the 4th to the 7th string. If you rest your picking hand on the bridge, you'll be able to quickly *roll* into the mutes. Strive for a taut, chunky tone, and snap those octave jumps.

Ex. 3

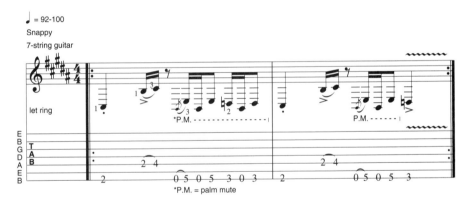

Sometimes it feels good to minimize fretting-hand fuss and simply focus on rhythmic drive. The chugging Ex. 4 is adapted from a riff played by Meegs Rascon in Coal Chamber's "Sway." (Rascon tunes his 6-string B.C. Rich to *BEADGB*—the bottom six strings of a 7-string—and he uses custom S.I.T. strings gauged .020, .026, .036, .046, .056, .070. All but the high *B* are wound.) Shoot for a grinding tone with plenty of upper-midrange sparkle, and if you're feeling adventurous, experiment with a slow flange. For an extra crisp finish, play those last two power chords staccato.

With its massive low *B*, the 7-string has a potent bottom end. But wait—there's more: Drop the 7th string down a whole-step (moving from *B* to *A*, as in Ex. 5) and prepare to be amazed. Related to the 6-string's dropped-*D* tuning, this 7-string, dropped-*A* tuning provides *serious* heaviosity to bands.

"We were one of the first bands to really get into 7-string," says Korn co-guitarist Brian "Head" Welch. "After a while we noticed that more people were playing 7-strings, so we thought, Let's go lower." Welch, who uses a .060 bottom string, tunes everything down a step from standard 7-string tuning (*ADGCFAD*), but you can play the next two examples using Ex. 5's dropped-*A* tuning.

Ex. 4

Ex. 5

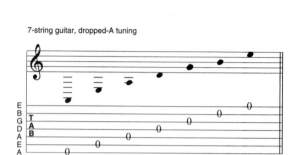

Example 6 is derived from Korn's "Counting." Like Ex. 4, this riff is about rhythmic power, not fancy fretwork. In fact, you need only one finger to grip these power chords. Make sure you *play* the eighth-note rests. Many guitarists seem impatient with silence and rush through it, but you can't create gut-wrenching lines when you're in a hurry. The challenge in this example is to weave the hammer, slides, and pickstrokes into a unified rhythm.

Ex. 6

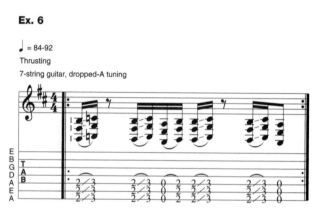

Korn's "Trash" inspired the moves in Ex. 7, another dropped-*A* crusher. The two half-step slides build harmonic tension, which is resolved in beat *one* of each measure. Don't forget the articulation details—the staccato mark (bar 1, beat one) and accents (bar 2, beats *two* and *four*).

Ex. 7

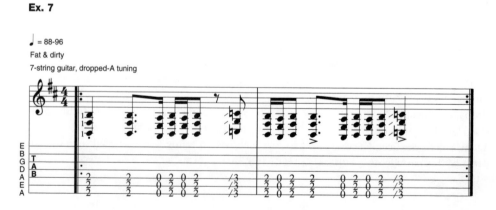

Many old-school power riffs sound cool on dropped-*A* 7-string. If you know such gems as "Train Kept a Rollin'" or "All Day and All of the Night," you'll dig how they sound transposed to 7-string. Take Ex. 8, which is recycled from Neil Young's "Cinnamon Girl." Played a 4th lower than it was written, the passage really takes off in bars 2 and 4 when the low *A* and *C* chords kick in. Mercy!

Ex. 8

Most of us don't utter the words "blues" and "7-string" in the same breath, but many classic blues riffs sound *killer* transposed to the 7-string's bottom register. Try Ex. 9—a low-slung take on Albert King's "Born Under a Bad Sign." When you hit that deep *D*—wow! In a juke joint, you could rattle bottles off the bar with this one note. The "bend 1/4" markings indicate a quarter-tone stretch. That's just enough to create emotional tension, but not enough to lift the pitch to the next fret. You'll feel when it's right.

Ex. 9

Example 10 shows how you can amble across the 7-string's wide fretboard to comp a bluesy IV7–I7–V7–I7 pattern in the key of *E*. The first two bars will sound familiar—you've probably played these moves many times on a 6-string. But when you reach bar 3, the low *B* string adds a new depth and power to this boogie figure. Play the passage fingerstyle, and again, watch the accents. See how they occur when you're squeezing two strings? As you practice this passage, think "pinch-*squeeze*, pinch-*squeeze*, pinch-*squeeze*."

Ex. 10

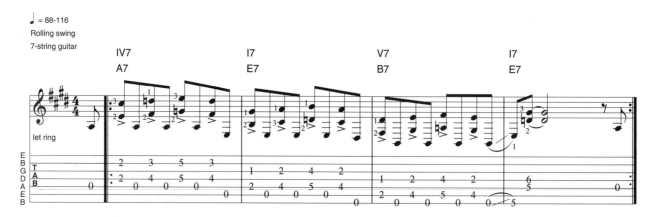

At times, learning an instrument can be frustrating. That's when you want to whip out something fun—like Ex. 11, a rumbling rendition of the theme from *Peter Gunn*. It's hard not to smile when you hear this riff bouncing off the bottom *B* string. Henry Mancini's original recording was pretty straight, but Dick Dale used quarter-bends to add sleaze to his version, so that's what we'll do in bar 2. For a surfy vibe, hit the bright switch, turn up the reverb, and use downstrokes on all the notes.

Ex. 11

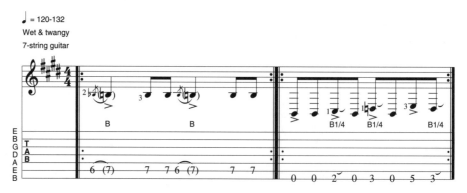

Once you've built some 7-string momentum, the challenge is to keep discovering new ideas. Here are a few areas to investigate:

- Extend your favorite scale patterns across the fretboard to include the 7th string.
- Select your coolest 6-string chord progressions and rework them for the 7-string. Find ways to incorporate the bottom *B* string in your voicings. For example, try moving notes that occur on the 5th (*A*) string down an octave by simply fingering them three frets lower on the 7th (*B*) string.
- Triads that lie on the standard guitar's 5th, 4th, and 3rd strings are fingered identically on its 6th, 5th, and 4th strings. This is because the guitar's bottom four strings (*EADG*) are tuned in uniform 4ths. On the 7-string guitar, this uniform-4ths tuning expands to include the 7th string and thus yields *three* matched string-sets: *B–E–A, E–A–D, A–D–G.* The payoff? You can immediately finger dozens of familiar triads (as well as arpeggios and intervals) on the 7th, 6th, and 5th strings once you visualize this relationship. Try it.

BLOOD SUGAR GROOVE MAGIC

The Red Hot Chili Peppers' Funky Punk Metal

John Frusciante

BY JOE GORE

In the early '80s the Red Hot Chili Peppers combined metal-style riffs (and volume) with funk-inspired grooves and punk sensibilities to produce a style that brought them stadium-level popularity and launched scores of imitators. The addition of guitarist John Frusciante (after the death of co-founder Hillel Slovak) for 1989's *Mother's Milk* sharpened the band's metal edge, but the groove remained king in the Peppers' high-impact sound.

We can't tell how to cop a Chili Pepper attitude, but we can help you cop some of their licks. The riff in Ex. 1a recalls Frusciante's guitar part in "Magic Johnson." It's heavy on offbeat 16th-notes, so watch your counting. John uses a lot of "scratching" in the style of James Brown guitarist Jimmy Nolen, and he varies his patterns quite a bit (Examples 1b–1c). In Ex. 1d the feel segues from James Brown funk to Metallica chunk as bar 2's 9th-chord stops lead to bar 3's octave *E*'s.

Ex. 1a

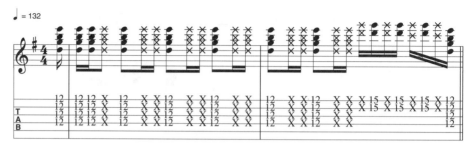

Ex. 1b

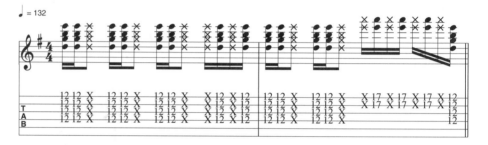

Ex. 1c

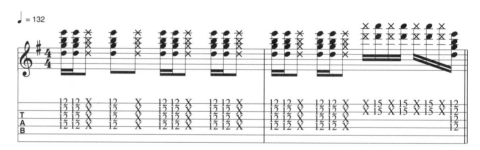

Ex. 1d

Examples 2a–2b show the Zeppelin/Hendrix vein of tunes like "Good Time Boys." To catch the feel you need to bash a bit, hitting the strings adjacent to the main notes for a percussive effect.

Ex. 2a

♩ = 96

Ex. 2b

♩ = 96

Paradoxically rawer yet more sophisticated than their previous albums, 1991's *Blood Sugar Sex Magik* boasted a new level of ensemble sensitivity for the Chilis. With Frusciante revealing a mature, egoless style, the band scaled heights of funkiness attained by such long-time groove models as P-Funk, the Meters, and Sly & the Family Stone.

Examples 3a–3c show a riff and variations you might hear on a tune like "Funky Monks." Frusciante plays this kind of riff very hard—those low-*E* snaps should really snarl.

Ex. 3a

Slow funk   Verse

Ex. 3b

Slow funk

Ex. 3c

Slow funk

Inspired by the intro to "Mellow Ship Slinky in *B* Major," Examples 4a–4b show a line Frusciante might play in parallel octaves with bassist Flea, bashing all six strings with his pick while carefully muting with his left hand. "It's good to use all downstrokes for that kind of part," Frusciante notes. Example 4c shows Frusciante's rhythm-guitar variation, while Ex. 5 lays out a percussive scratch riff in 4ths, à la "If You Have to Ask."

For Ex. 6a lower your high *E* string to *E*♭ to get the sound of Frusciante's clangy main riff on "The Power of Equality," and bash and damp with maximum brutality for the chorus riff in Ex. 6b. If your knuckles aren't bleeding, you're probably not playing hard enough.

Ex. 4a

Ex. 4b

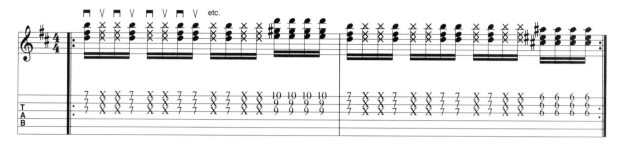

Ex. 4c

Ex. 5

Medium funk with slight swing

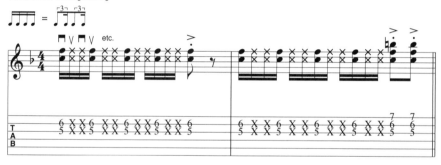

Ex. 6a

Up funk

Ex. 6b

Up funk

OLD RIFFS, NEW TRICKS

A Lesson with Jerry Cantrell

BY JAMES ROTONDI & JOE GORE

Ozzy! Ozzy! Ozzy!" Thundering cheers shake the backstage area at the Kansas Coliseum where Jerry Cantrell, having finished Alice in Chains' opening slot, is getting ready to show me some of the patented riffs he calls "chunge"—Cantrell's goof on "grunge." While Cantrell's sonic vocabulary is cut from classic metal—Sabbath, Zeppelin, Aerosmith, AC/DC—he puts artful twists on stock lead and chord forms with funky dissonances and offbeat time signatures.

Played in dropped-*D* tuning (just tune your low *E* string down a whole-step), Ex. 1a recalls the brutal main chorus part to *Dirt*'s "Dam That River." The riff is in 6/4 time, which like 4/4 has a straight duple-meter backbeat feel. Note: For extra weight, Cantrell and Alice in Chains tuned down a half-step, but for simplicity we've notated the examples at standard pitch.

Ex. 1a

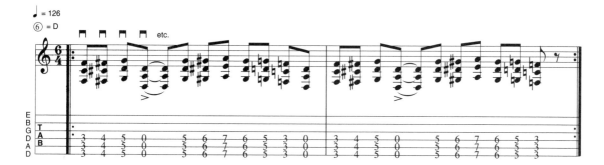

Example 1b is the single-note line played over Ex. 1a. Cantrell intuitively avoids relying on the tonic *D*, opting instead to fashion a hook from the 3rd and ♭7th scale tones—*F* and *C*—lending the part more harmonic richness. Like Ex. 1b, Ex. 1c's verse riff plays off the *F–C* open-5th power chord. The riff has more of a 4/4 phrasing, so we've notated it that way.

Ex. 1b

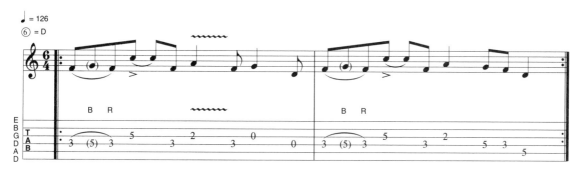

Ex. 1c

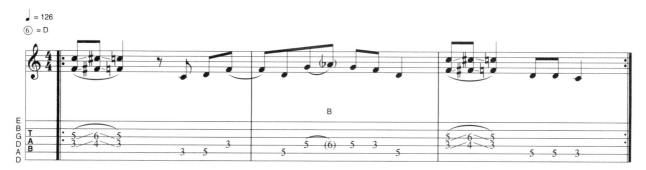

Once you've tuned your 6th string back up, try Ex. 2's insidious riff, which recalls the opening of "Go Smack." Full of chromatic slip-sliding, the riff's key is ambiguous. Cantrell shows his rhythmic savvy by his unexpected eighth-note rests. Laying the side of your right palm against the bridge as you chunk along gives this riff its mischievous muted quality.

Ex. 2

The explosive passage in Ex. 3a is ultra percussive, and Cantrell's fingering makes it a good all-purpose fingering exercise. As Jerry alternates between the initial two power chords, he fingers the *F#* with his 1st and 3rd fingers and the *C* with his 2nd and 4th. The riff recalls "Sickman," which Cantrell describes as "the most fucked-up piece of music I could write."

Ex. 3a

In Ex. 3b Cantrell works the *Eb/A* tritone up the neck in three inversions, each six frets above the last, as he does in the 3/4 bridge section of "Sickman." In Ex. 3c Jerry arpeggiates the same dissonant harmonies, using his 3rd and 4th fingers on the 4th and 3rd strings respectively. Sick—really sick.

Ex. 3b

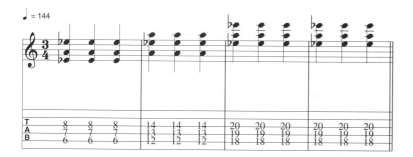

Ex. 3c

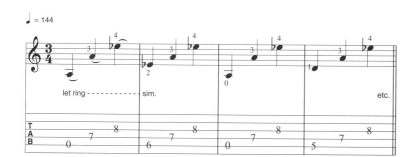

TWEAK SHOW

Kirk Hammett on Riff Mutation

BY JOE GORE

Metallica's basic unit of musical currency is the riff. All four members contribute to the riff bank, though it's usually bandleaders James Hetfield and Lars Ulrich who stitch the choicest bits into fixed structures, much the way Doc Frankenstein assembled monsters from miscellaneous body parts. Kirk Hammett has generated some of the band's most memorable guitar figures, including the signature pattern from the group's biggest hit, "Enter Sandman."

Hammett finds himself increasingly cast as composer/texturalist rather than grandstanding soloist. "I'm really not interested in proving myself in that fashion anymore," he asserts. "My main motivation is just working in the context of what we're trying to communicate." For that reason, we decided to bypass the usual licks 'n' tricks approach in this lesson in favor of exploring how Kirk concocts and mutates his riffs.

"Let's try taking the seed of an idea and expanding on it," says Kirk, grabbing a crusty-stringed ESP and perching on the edge of his bed. He starts to pick, immediately gravitating to Ex. 1a, a figure that emphasizes the low open-*E* (or *E♭*) string, as Metallica licks are wont to do.

Ex. 1a

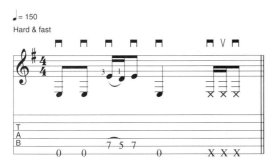

"I look for a group of notes that sounds interesting but still organic and natural. Sometimes riffs sound too forced. I look for ones that flow and have a good groove. I like riffs that sound slightly familiar, but not completely. Sometimes I play something, and someone says, 'It sounds like something I've heard before.' A lot of players would say 'Fuck it,' but I'm more likely to think, 'Good—I'm on the right track.' It's good if it locks on to a feeling you've felt before from some other type of music. I consciously look for things like that."

Are the ideas ever too generic? Does he ever have to tweak them or add kinks? "Sure—I tweak them a lot. When I'm writing a lick or riff, I'll play it like 50 times, but, say, change it every fourth time. Maybe I'll alter it rhythmically, or go from a minor 3rd to a major 3rd, or sharp the 4. Maybe I'll add drone notes or play it on the upbeat. I might chop it in half, add bends—there are so many different ways of doing it." He resumes the pattern and begins to morph it, trying out the variations in Examples 1b through 1e. He adds assorted double-stops and accents, but most interesting is the way he displaces the rhythm, exploring how it sounds to move the 5th-string accent that initially fell on beat *two* and ultimately situating it on the downbeat.

Ex. 1b

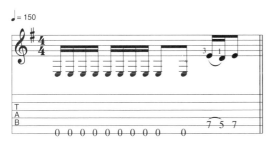

Ex. 1c

Ex. 1d

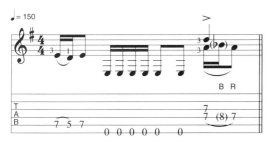

Ex. 1e

Next Kirk extends the idea into a four-bar unit that deviates from the basic pattern in the final measure (Ex. 2). "James and I both do that a lot," Hammett notes. "Like 'Enter Sandman,' which repeats the basic one-measure riff but adds a tail to make a four-bar phrase. Going to the ♭5 like this is very natural for me. It adds that dark tension."

Ex. 2

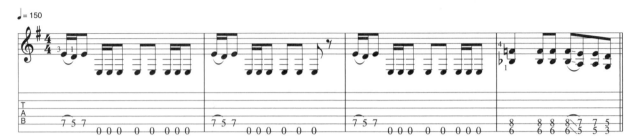

Okay, maybe this off-the-cuff idea isn't the greatest riff of Kirk's career, but if he were trying to develop it, what sort of secondary patterns might be set against it? "The first things that spring to mind are octave patterns," he replies, improvising Ex. 3a while I hold down Ex. 1e on Kirk's Parker. He expands on the octave idea with Ex. 3b, adding 16th-note syncopations that lend an entirely new feel. Kirk continues the syncopation with Ex. 3c, a stock funk figure that works surprisingly well against the heavy pattern.

Ex. 3a

Ex. 3b

Ex. 3c

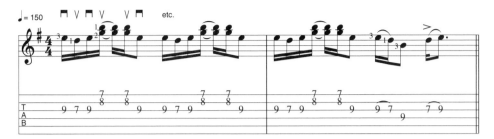

What about thickening the basic part, as opposed to playing against it? "If I wanted to make it really heavy, I'd drop the low *E* to *D*, doubling the main accent an octave below and playing half-muted on the rest of the pattern [Ex. 4a]." Finally Kirk retunes the 6th string and grinds out the low, chomping pattern in Ex. 4b, which dovetails with the initial figure, adding a mighty backbeat lift without overshadowing the basic riff. No earthshaking innovation, but a strong, solid texture that sounds quite tough even on unplugged electrics and is very much in keeping with Metallica's lean and deceptively effortless aesthetic.

Ex. 4a

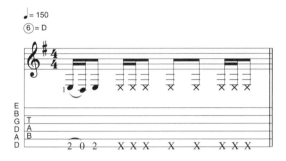

Ex. 4b

RUNNING DOWN A DREAM

Marty Friedman Shares the Riffs & Inspiration Behind *Music for Speeding*

BY JUDE GOLD

Being a good guitar player is dangerous," asserts Marty Friedman, "because if you have chops, people will want to hire you."

Whoa, wait a second. Since when was getting paid good money to play guitar anything less than one of the highest aspirations? After all, whether you're touring with a national act, playing gigs around town, putting guitar parts on jingles and soundtracks, or doing album sessions, doesn't paying your rent doing music beat a regular 9-to-5er?

"Don't get me wrong," says Friedman. "Being able to make any kind of living at all in music is like winning the lottery. But if you're a good player, it's so friggin' easy to get caught up doing gigs and making money that it takes you away from your *own* musical vision. There's a big difference between being good at playing music and being good at *making* music. Getting your songs realized—taking them from ideas and demos up to actually being on an album—is an entirely different process from that of learning your instrument."

For Friedman, as much as he loves playing on other people's projects, all side gigs are a means to help him evolve his own sound. And with one spin of his 2003 album *Music for Speeding*, it's obvious that his sound is headed into the future.

Powering this collection of adrenaline-soaked instrumentals is the high-octane, bone-crushing lead guitar that made Friedman famous as Megadeth's

FREE Audio Version Online

PlayMetal.TrueFire.com

lead guitarist. However, it's the many *new* sonic elements that make this record so entrancing. Friedman delivers a kaleidoscopic range of guitar and synth-guitar tones, roller-coaster dynamic shifts, hypnotic loops and techno textures, and even a disco beat or two. But what really gives the record its rock 'n' roll muscle is an arsenal of new riffs—many of which Friedman is about to show you here—that are as catchy and melodic as they are vicious.

"To be 1,000 percent honest with you, guitar music bores me to tears," Friedman reveals. "We've all heard the sound of guitar for many years, and the sound alone is not enough to hold my attention. I need a good *song* to make me happy. The challenge for me was to make a guitar record that even non-guitar fans are going to dig."

Making someone feel good with your music, however, implies that they're actually listening to it. One way Friedman catches listeners' attention is by hitting them over the head with monstrous riffs such as Ex. 1, which opens "Salt in the Wound." This simple lick involves two power 5ths, *E5* and *F5*, a touch of palm-muting on the open *E* notes that land between the 5ths, and a Godzilla-sized distortion sound.

For maximum thrash, Friedman suggests remaining *in position* for the first bar of this lick (which repeats three times). With this approach, you play *E5* with the low string open and the 2nd finger squeezing the 2nd fret of the 5th string. When *F5* hits on beat *two*, instead of moving your fretting hand one fret higher up the neck, simply fret the interval with your 1st and 4th fingers as indicated.

"It's not only easier to play that way, but it sounds cleaner too, because it cuts down on finger noise. This is definitely a Megadeth style of lick, though I don't think Megadeth would have done the sliding chords in the second half."

Now that you've got people listening, try to *keep* them listening. For Friedman, this can be as easy as playing the simplest riff from "Salt in the Wound," the machine-gun texture in Ex. 2. "This *should* be really easy to play," he says of the rapid-fire 16th-notes on the low

Ex. 1

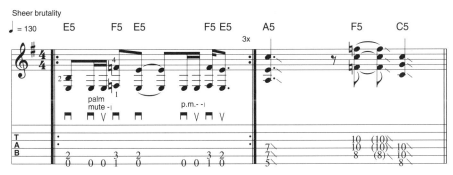

Ex. 2

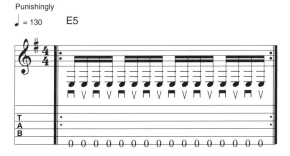

string, "but it's harder than it seems. The challenge is playing it so evenly that it has a hypnotic sound. You want it to sound like a helicopter."

The lick then morphs, becoming Ex. 3. In this riff, the 16th-note *E*-string assault continues, but he adds strategically placed 1st-to-2nd finger hammer-ons on the same string to give the riff a more jagged, melodic contour. "It's still fairly simple, but there's a big difference between playing it well and playing it like a *god*."

Ex. 3

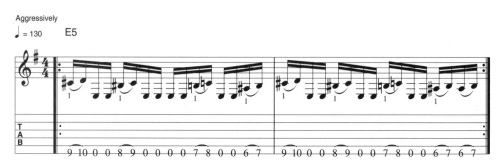

When it comes to writing hard-rocking licks, few guitarists—unless they have significant blues roots—use both the major and minor tones the way Friedman does in Ex. 4, which is the opening lick to "Gimme a Dose." This aggressive riff peaks with a *C–C♯–C* move on the 3rd string, tagging the ♭3, the ♮3, and then the ♭3 again in the key of *A*.

With the last three chords in this example, Friedman creates a gargantuan, almost detuned sound by doubling the 5ths in a *D5–D♭5–C5*. For instance, in the *D5* chord (bar 2, beat *two*), the 5 (*A*) appears in the upper *and* lower voice, while the root (*D*) remains sandwiched in between. "Playing it that way adds some serious *cojones*."

Ex. 4

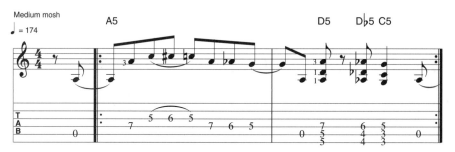

If there's one "detuned" moment worth checking out on *Music for Speeding*, it's the intro to "Catfight" that starts with the merciless mosh of Ex. 5. Although it's actually played in dropped-*C* standard tuning, you can easily play it as presented here—that is, in dropped-*D*—by lowering your 6th string a whole-step from standard. This makes the bottom three strings spell a meaty *D5* chord. Because the riff is all open strings, the goal is to create exciting dynamics by applying palm muting between the chords as indicated.

The next lick you hear on "Catfight" is the groovin' Phrygian motif in Ex. 6. "That's Phrygian?" asks Friedman, not one to place too much import on naming scales and modes. "There's no one scale that's going to make you sound one way or the other—it's all about

Ex. 5

Mercilessly

♩ = 126

Dropped-D tuning

⑥ = D   D5

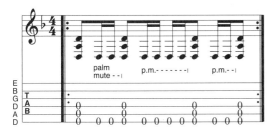

Ex. 6

With adrenaline

♩ = 126

Dropped-D tuning

⑥ = D   D5

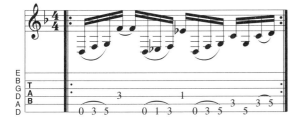

phrases. Actually, I originally heard this phrase as a synth line—the type of thing you might hear on a techno track. I wanted to record it on guitar, but it sounded so natural on synth, I eventually played it on both."

These days, Friedman rarely uses the stock pickups on his Ibanez guitars, opting instead for the powerful range of guitar sounds he gets running his Roland VG-88 guitar synthesizer/modeling system into the clean channel of his 300-watt Crate BV300H. ("That head has clean, solid power for days!") And although Friedman strings his guitars with D'Addarios, gauged .010–.052, the VG-88 allows him to change tunings on the fly.

"The days of having to switch guitars for each tuning are over. All I have to do is step on a pedal, and I'm in whatever tuning I want to be in. And the *tones*! Roland has modeled all the amps, and when you hear this thing, you'd never in your wildest dreams think it was anything but a screaming guitar."

"I could go on for hours about the music in Japan," says Friedman, who is fluent in Japanese. The guitarist fell in love with Japan and its culture the first time he visited, playing in Cacophony alongside his friend and fellow shredder Jason Becker in the late '80s. "Pop, rock, and even hard rock over there are much more uplifting, happy, and melodic than what you get in America. I mean, America *is* the best country in the world, but it seems like everybody who writes hard, aggressive music here is complaining about how horrible life is. In Japan, instead of depressing lyrics and images that are dark and ugly, the scene is all about hot chicks, well-dressed dudes, and amazing cutting-edge music production. It's a different world."

You now understand the inspiration behind "Cheer Girl Rampage," a song that tries to capture the upbeat roar of electronic music pouring onto Tokyo streets from the city's gaming parlors. In Ex. 7, you'll find the melodic climax of the song, a string of triplets that wildly ascends up the neck. There are two basic moves involved in this phrase—the first six notes and the last six notes in bar 1. Once you've learned the twists and turns, move onto bar 2, where the same pattern recurs a whole-step higher, and then continue taking it up the neck from there.

"This is very typical of the things Jason and I would play together," recalls Friedman, who, on January 1, 2003, performed Becker's electric guitar concerto with a full orchestra in San Francisco. Though unable to perform because of ALS (Lou Gehrig's disease), Becker was in attendance. "The whole thing was a huge thrill for me," says Friedman.

"There's a lot of ripping guitar on *Music for Speeding*, and I'm very proud of it, but at the same time, I know there's going to be someone saying, 'Oh man, that's just another guitar dude wanking,'" says Friedman. "So as sort of a tongue-in-cheek joke on guitar records, I recorded '0-7-2'—which is about 40 seconds of super-fast classical wanking. The joke is that is if you say oh-seven-two in Japanese it sounds very similar to the Japanese word for masturbation."

Ex. 7

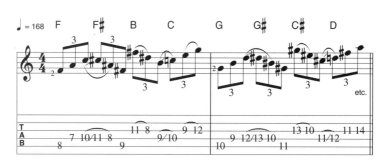

Example 8 presents opening measures of "0-7-2." "It's loosely based on a live solo I used to do in Megadeth," he explains. "I tracked it in a very interesting way—I step-recorded it using MIDI. I could have just recorded it conventionally, playing it straight through, but

Ex. 8

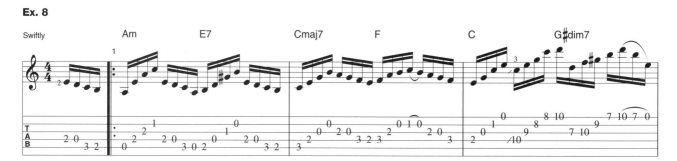

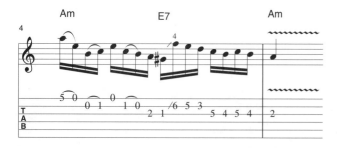

doing it in MIDI allowed me to stack four instruments instantly. You're hearing piano, acoustic guitar, and two violin samples."

Despite his disdain for "wanking," Friedman has nothing against head-turning guitar licks. "You have to make the show-off stuff actually *mean* something, so it's not just a mindless display of technique. If you just play something fast and tricky by itself, it means nothing, and your music will have an amateurish sound. But if you do it right when someone's attention is piqued—like after building up dynamically to a climax in the song—*that's* when you hit them with some bitchin' lick."

As the intro to "Ripped" proves, you can also *open* a song with a climactic phrase, and drop in the intensity later on. "I think the use of dynamics is what has most evolved in popular music over the last ten years." Example 9 shows how "Ripped" bursts out of the gate with an onslaught of *E* minor 16th-notes.

Ex. 9

"I don't like that real even *diddly diddly* sound you get when 16ths are played in groups of four or eight—it's too predictable. I like to group them in odd numbers—which puts accents in different places. It's still a big stream of 16ths, but it sounds a lot more interesting. Just be careful not to lose track of the downbeats. I actually doubled this part an octave higher, playing it like this [Ex. 10]."

Ex. 10

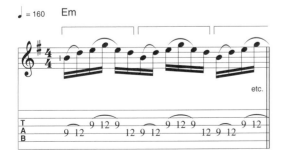

"This is going to be hard to say to all those good guitarists who are always practicing, but I'll just hit them with it—*stop* practicing so damn much. There are only 24 hours in a day, and if you want to get your music out there, use any extra time and money you have to make demos of every one of your ideas. Everything has got to revolve around getting your music done. Of course, you should still do outside session work and gigs, but when you're out there working, use those opportunities to make contacts with people you may someday want to use on *your* project.

"A lot of what I learned from [Megadeth founder] Dave Mustaine is how to keep the final vision in mind. Mustaine is a great guitar player—he has a trademark heavy-riff thing that nobody can touch—but he's so much more than a guitarist. He knew he had to get people onboard with him—like a melodic lead guitarist, and that was *me*—to make the music come together just as he heard it in his head. I think everyone who successfully writes and records music always envisions the final project, and everything else is just a means to get there."

DOMO ARIGATO MR. VIBRATO

Vibrato is easy, right? Nothing to it—just squeeze a note, wiggle your fretting finger, and *voilà*! "But vibrato is deceptively simple," counters Marty Friedman. "It's a stumbling point for a lot of guitarists because they don't actually listen to their vibrato. Instead, they play this forced-sounding, shrill, spastic vibrato. Even if you're just putting vibrato on one held note [Fig. 1], your vibrato should come from within you, so that your finger can really sing the note you want it to sing.

Fig. 1

"In some cases no vibrato is best, especially if the melody is simple and your guitar is in tune and well-intonated. Or, you might want to hold a note for several beats and then add vibrato, as good singers often do [Fig. 2]."

Friedman often likes to apply vibrato to bent notes—specifically, pre-bent notes, such as those in Fig. 3, which starts on a pre-bent A at the 6th fret of the 4th string. "The second I pick it, I drop it down a half-step and then immediately back up. The key is making the note go down and up so quickly that you hardly hear the dip in pitch. Instead you just hear a note that seems to jump out at you. Then, add vibrato. Also, notice how I'm originating from notes that most people wouldn't start on in the key of *A* minor—namely, *G#* and *A#*. They're supposedly 'wrong' notes, but if you dip into them for just a split second, they sound cool."

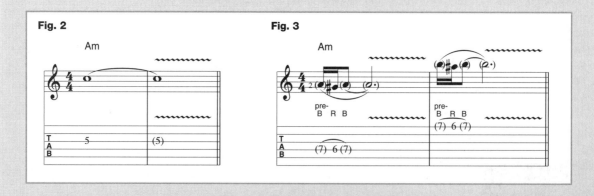

Fig. 2

Fig. 3

JUST DO EVERYTHING!

A Lesson with Nuno Bettencourt

BY JESSE GRESS

Nuno Bettencourt's fretboard wizardry provides blueprints for sonic architecture far beyond the realm of cliché. On albums like Extreme's *III Sides to Every Story* Nuno coalesces his talents and his bandmates' around a funky, hard-hitting, and melodic songwriting approach that owes as much to the Beatles, Sly & the Family Stone, and Todd Rundgren's Utopia as it does to Led Zeppelin. Nuno insists his musical goals have little to do with fretboard pyrotechnics. "A lot of people get caught up in too much guitar," Nuno notes. "They don't realize that your technique, your writing, your inspiration, is just not going to be from the instrument—it's too obvious that way. If you listen to piano or any other instrument enough, you'll spit it out on your guitar somehow. That's what makes for interesting musicians—how they graft styles from other instruments onto theirs."

Nuno's intuitive sense of rhythm shines through on heavy, low-register single-note riffs, chord progressions, countermelodies, and solos. "I still play a lot of drums. When I play guitar, it's very rhythmic and drum-oriented. It just runs through me."

One of Nuno's signatures is lacing single-note low-register riffs with funky 16th-note syncopations. "With funky stuff like 'Cupid's Dead' and 'Politicalamity' (from *III Sides to Every Story*), it's what you do with your right hand that counts. It's like there's a clock going all the time, even during solos." Nuno demonstrates by picking a constant stream of 16th-note muted-string "chucks" with strictly alternating downstrokes and upstrokes. He then plays Ex. 1 without breaking the flow, even for rests or tied beats. (Note: Nuno always tunes down a half-step for maximum heavyosity, but all examples are notated a half-step above their actual pitch to reflect his fingerings.) The quarter- and eighth-notes fall naturally on downstrokes, while the in-between 16th-notes fall on upstrokes (one exception: the 16th-note triplet in bar 2 is picked down-up-down). The muted "chucks" are an important part of the overall sound of this and similar figures.

Ex. 1

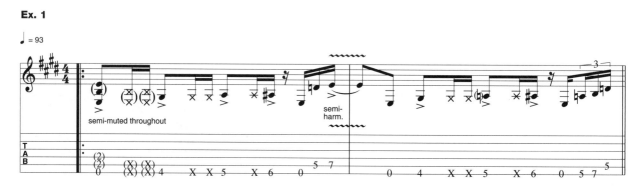

The single-note riff in Ex. 2 is designed to contrast sharply to the Beatlesesque string quartet that opens "Rest in Peace." It exemplifies "playing to the clock" in a higher register. Use your neck pickup and go for a Hendrix vibe.

Ex. 2

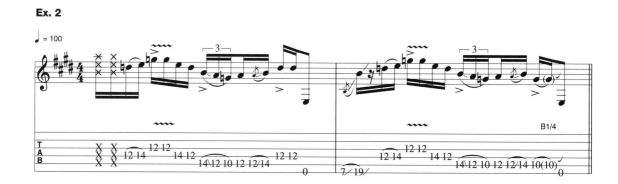

Another item in Nuno's bag of rhythm tricks is displacement—that is, repeating a melodic figure, but shifting it in time so the accents fall on different beats of the measure. Study the displacement in Ex. 3: The *E–D–B–G* descending arpeggio begins on the downbeat of bar 1, and then moves to the upbeat beat *four*. Meanwhile, bar 2's ascending *E–E–A–B–D* lick gets sliced and diced in bar 3, with the repeated 16th-note *E*'s shifted to the back end of beat *two*.

Ex. 3

Unexpected open strings find their way into many signature Bettencourt riffs, as seen in Examples 4 and 5.

Ex. 4

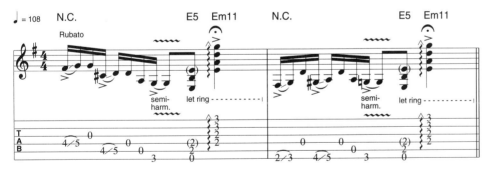

Ex. 5

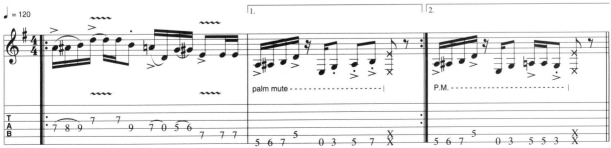

Sometimes Nuno outlines chords with repeated 16th-note patterns. In Ex. 6 he conveys the underlying chord progression simply by changing the first note of each pattern.

Ex. 6

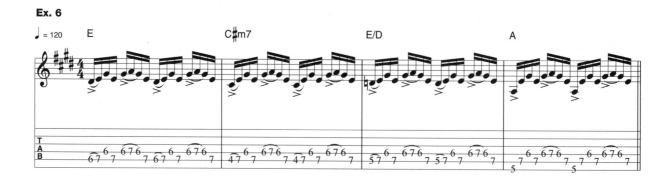

One of Nuno's personal rut-busters is to bypass the standard "blues box" (Fig. 1) in favor of the symmetrical pentatonic-minor fingering pattern that lies just below it (Fig. 2). We've shown both examples in *E*; the "common" box position is located at the 12th fret, Nuno's version at the 9th. "I used to play the higher position all the time, but then I looked for something to add life to that, so there's always somewhere to go."

The short but memorable fill in Ex. 7 milks this pattern for a cool string-skipping sequence that includes the non-scale ♮3 and ♭5. "When you create something you're just playing what you hear. There's not really any recipe. I always try to tell people, 'Don't be a guitar player—be a musician. Just do everything.'"

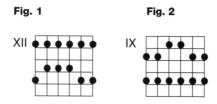

Fig. 1   **Fig. 2**

Ex. 7

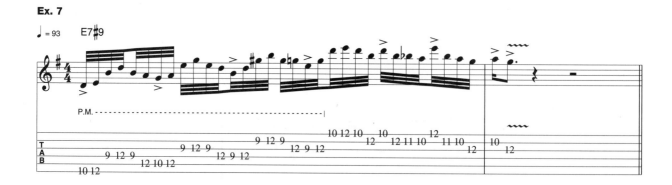

RITCHIE BLACKMORE

Playing with Electricity

BY JESSE GRESS

Ritchie Blackmore may be the link between the great blues-based rockers of the '60s and the diatonic shredders of the '80s. The unique hybrid of blues-rock idioms and quasi-classical modal and harmonic minor sounds he developed during his years with Deep Purple and Rainbow grew out of Hendrix, Page, and Beck while anticipating Van Halen and Malmsteen, and their countless imitators.

Influenced by Big Jim Sullivan, Scotty Moore, James Burton, Duane Eddy, and Les Paul, Blackmore started out as a session player with the Outlaws and Screaming Lord Sutch before joining the original Deep Purple lineup in 1968. The band's early-'70s incarnation may have been the prototype heavy metal band. The band's albums *In Rock*, *Fireball*, *Machine Head*, and *Made in Japan*, all recorded between '70 and '73, remain landmarks of the genre, epitomized to this day by the Blackmore power chords that open "Smoke on the Water."

Long identified as a Strat cat, Blackmore actually used a Gibson ES-335 on the first two Purple albums before making the switch midway through the third and embarking on his radical tremolo bar approach. He also switched from Vox AC30 amps to customized Marshalls that he claimed pushed 500-plus watts. (Did I mention that Ritchie likes it loud?)

Blackmore says a year of early classical training influenced his compositional sense

and contributed to the extraordinary dexterity of his left-hand pinky. But structured study never diminished Blackmore's penchant for musical risk-taking. "The art of chance music is knowing what to do if you don't get what you first tried for," he told *Guitar Player* back in 1972. "That's what interests me—playing with electricity."

The following examples show some of Blackmore's favorite musical building blocks. Example 1a illustrates how Ritchie favors spicing up pentatonic minor runs with the #4/♭5 scale degree (*D#*), often hitting the note straight on rather than bending into it. The 6 (*F#*) gives the bluesy lick in Ex. 1b a Dorian slant.

Ex. 1a

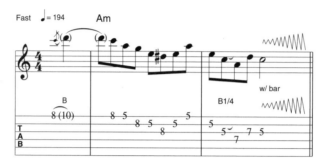

Ex. 1b

Another passing tone, the 7th (*A*), appears in Ex. 2, which combines all of the above elements to lead into an introductory V chord. The brief bend into the 3 (*D#*) blurs the line between major and minor. In fact the only missing chromatic scale degrees are ♭2, 2, and ♭6. Example 3 has a definite Dorian vibe, but also emphasizes the #4 (*E#*). And ♭2, a darker Phrygian element, appears briefly in Ex. 4.

Ex. 2

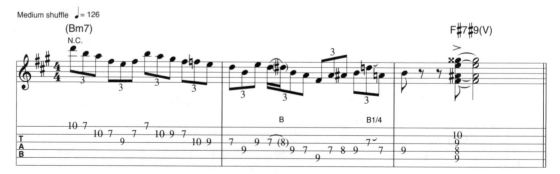

Ex. 3

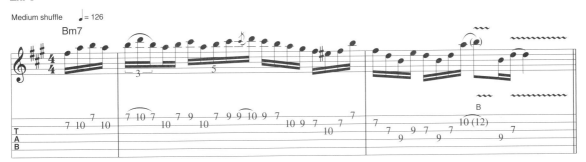

Ex. 4

The short *A* minor ostinatos in Examples 5a–5c appear often in Blackmore solos. Ritchie is also fond of moving the entire patterns (especially Ex. 5c's) up and down the neck in half-steps. The bluesy riff in Ex. 5d introduces a rhythmic variation, while Ex. 5e adds the Aeolian/natural minor ♭6 (*F*).

Ex. 5a   **Ex. 5b**   **Ex. 5c**

Ex. 5d   **Ex. 5e**

The pure *A* Phrygian run in Ex. 6 makes a great pinky-development exercise. The minor/add 9 arpeggio and ensuing bend in Ex. 7 lead to a cross-rhythm figure that momentarily implies 3/8 time. And Blackmore plays the ascending triplet arpeggios in Ex. 8 using strict alternate picking—no easy feat. Try harmonizing this line in diatonic 3rds and 5ths.

Ex. 6

Ex. 7

Ex. 8

The descending arpeggios in Ex. 9 incorporate bends into a Bach-influenced progression. Ex. 10 treats the same progression with a speedy, ascending motif that works its way up the *E* string diatonically, then descends via chromatic pull-offs over an open *E* pedal. Again, Blackmore's alternate picking approaches the superhuman.

Ex. 9

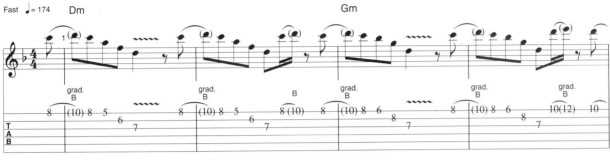

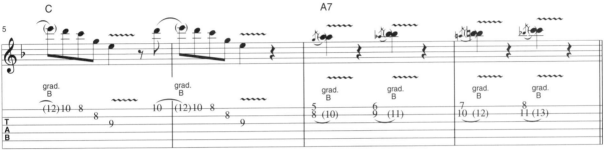

Ex. 10

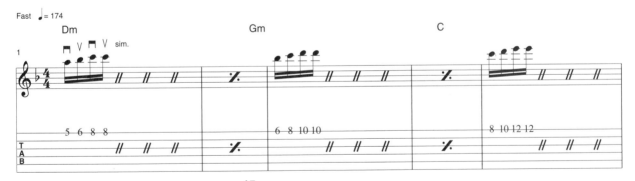

A Gypsy-flavored ensemble line from the Rainbow era, Ex. 11 relies entirely on the *E* harmonic minor scale (*E–F#–G–A–B–C–D#–E*) to play through the V–Im progression. (The Phrygian dominant mode, beloved by '80s neo-classical rockers, is built from the 5th scale degree of the harmonic minor scale: *B Phrygian dominant = B–C–D#–E–F#–G–A–B*.)

Ex. 11

The first two bars of Ex. 12 outline Im (*Gm*) and IVm (*Cm*) of *G* minor, blending *G* Aeolian and blues lines before shifting to *C* Aeolian and harmonic minor ideas. Ritchie treats each chord separately; *C* minor becomes a temporary tonal center, not just the subdominant (IVm) of *G* minor. The cool *D7* arpeggiations in bar 3 come from the *G* harmonic minor scale. The ♭2/♭9 degree (*E♭*) adds extra tension, and the concluding phrase is pure Bach 'n' roll.

Ex. 12

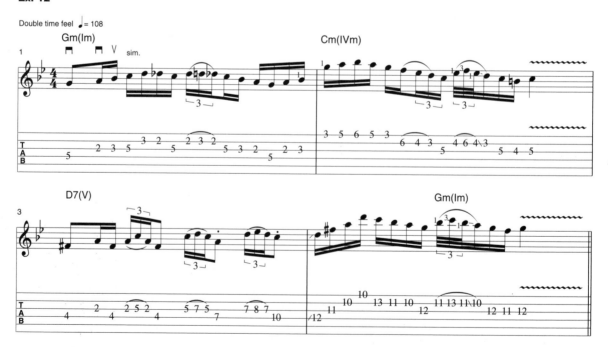

ZEPPELINEAGE

The Roots of Jimmy Page

BY JESSE GRESS

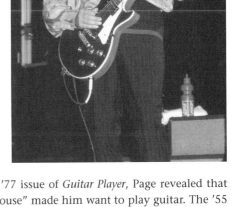

I n the liner notes to Led Zeppelin's *The Song Remains the Same* soundtrack, director Cameron Crowe recalls one of the band's legendary post-concert getaways. On board their touring plane, the stage-weary musicians collapsed around a video of Little Richard belting out "Tutti Frutti" in the 1957 film *The Girl Can't Help It*. Jimmy Page raised a toast: "No escaping our roots."

Page has bequeathed countless riffs and melodic ideas to subsequent generations of rock guitarists. Unlike the players who have tried to replicate his sound, however, Page never settled for merely copying his predecessors. His genius was to channel his influences into his own distinctive voice.

Let's explore some of the ingredients of Led Zeppelin's sonic stew. In the July '77 issue of *Guitar Player*, Page revealed that hearing Elvis Presley's "Baby, Let's Play House" made him want to play guitar. The '55 side features Scotty Moore playing a sparkly, alternating-bass rockabilly rhythm (Ex. 1), and Page breaks into a similar figure about nine minutes into the live version of "Whole Lotta Love" from *The Song Remains the Same*.

Ex. 1

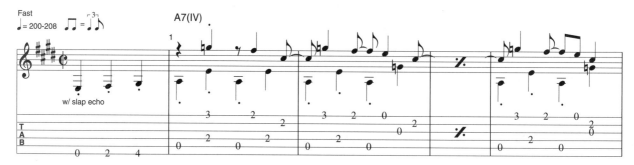

In concert, Zeppelin often used "Whole Lotta Love" and "Communication Breakdown" as the basis for extended jams that would include oldies such as "That's Alright Mama," "(You're So Square) Baby, I Don't Care," "Long Tall Sally," and "Whole Lotta Shakin' Goin' On." You can hear the influence of rockabilly guitar greats James Burton, Cliff Gallup, and Johnny Meeks in vintage-style Zep tunes like "Candy Store Rock" and "Ozone Baby."

A Les Paul disciple since his early teens, Jimmy was drawn as much to Paul's playing as to his multi-tracking techniques. "Fantastic!" he raved to *Guitar Player* about Paul's "It's Been a Long, Long, Time," a mid-'40s tune recorded with Bing Crosby. "It's everything in one go, and it's just one guitar!" Paul's style at the time embraced just about every technique then known to guitardom, including vibrato, hammer-ons, pull-offs, even feedback. His version of "Lady Be Good" (recorded with pianist Art Tatum and available on Tatum's *Piano Mastery)* features some wicked trills and pull-offs (Ex. 2). Listen to Page's "Heartbreaker" solo and the break 47 seconds into "Moby Dick" (both from *Led Zeppelin II)* and dig the conceptual similarities.

Ex. 2

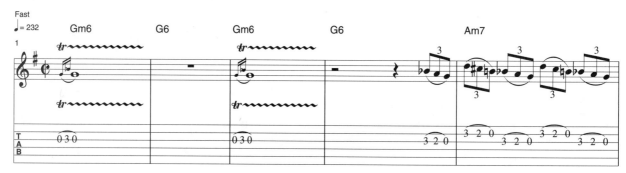

Ex. 2 cont.

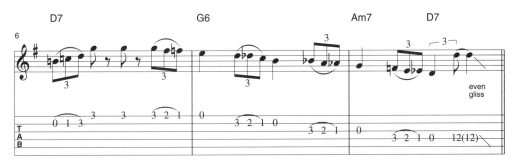

The blues played perhaps the largest role in shaping Jimmy's style, even in his pre-Zeppelin days. The Yardbirds' *Little Games,* an important transitional album, not only made several nods to blues greats, but also contained nuggets that would soon be polished into sections of Led Zeppelin songs—compare the solo on "Think About It" with the one on Zep's "Dazed and Confused." "Smile on Me" not only recalls Otis Rush's "All Your Love," but Page actually paraphrases Eric Clapton's break from the Bluesbreakers' version. "Drinking Muddy Water" is an all-out tribute to both Muddy Waters' "Rollin' and Tumblin, Part I" (Ex. 3) and Howlin' Wolf's "Down in the Bottom." (Note: In all capoed examples tab numbers represent actual fret positions.)

Ex. 3

Muddy sidemen like Luther Tucker, Pat Hare, Jimmy Rogers, and Buddy Guy all had their impact on Page. Muddy's version of Willy Dixon's "You Need Love" was definitely the model for the melody and lyrics to "Whole Lotta Love." And although Earl Hooker played slide on "You Shook Me," Page's intro to the tune on *Led Zeppelin* seems to owe more to Muddy's intros to "The Things That I Used to Do" and "My Home Is in the Delta," which Chess anthologized on the *Muddy Waters* box set.

Just as the Rolling Stones saw themselves as children of Muddy Waters and Chuck Berry, Led Zeppelin considered themselves sons of Howlin' Wolf. Robert Plant would string together titles of Dixon/Wolf tunes in his vocal improvisations ("Shake for me, I wanna be your back door man"), while Page tweaked "Killing Floor" into "The Lemon Song." Piece together the tune's full 12-bar progression by playing Ex. 4a followed by Ex. 4b. (The pickup to Ex. 4b replaces the last beat on the repeat of Ex. 4a.) Return to the I chord by playing Ex. 4a without the repeat, and then replace the last beat with the pickup into Ex. 4c. Transposing the bass line to *E* and playing under a high-*E* pedal yields the signature riff of "The Lemon Song."

Ex. 4a

* Play grace notes 1st time only.

Ex. 4b

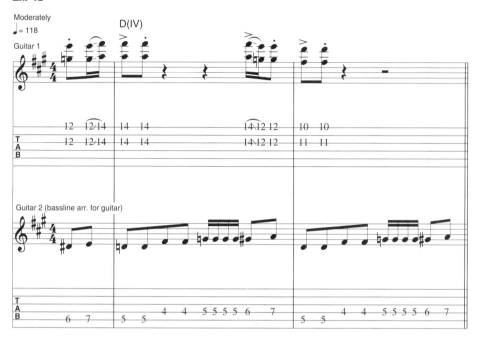

Ex. 4c

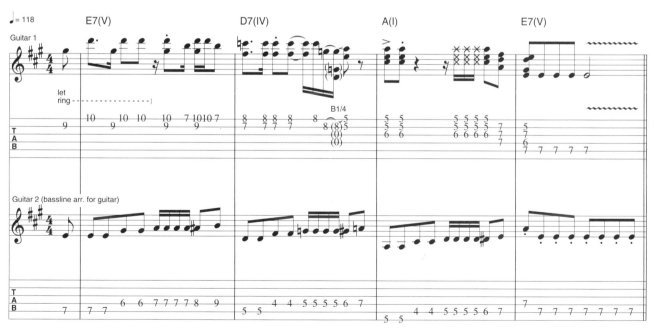

Many Wolf songs are based on just one chord; compare Zep's "How Many More Times" with Wolf's "How Many More Years," "Moaning for My Baby," and "You Gonna Wreck My Life" (available on the Chess *Howlin' Wolf* box set). Zeppelin's "The Rover" recalls Waters and Wolf, while "Bring It on Home" pays homage to Sonny Boy Williamson.

The playing of B.B., Albert, and Freddie King also echoes through Page's solos. Jimmy paraphrases B.B.'s fluid, swinging style for a few choruses of an uptempo shuffle beginning at 10:32 of the "Whole Lotta Love" jam (Examples 5a and 5b).

Ex. 5a

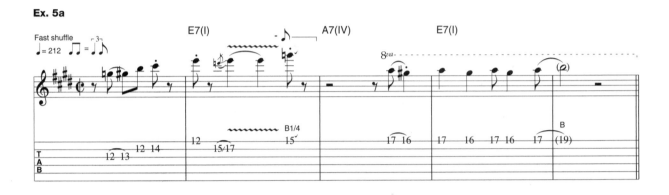

Ex. 5b

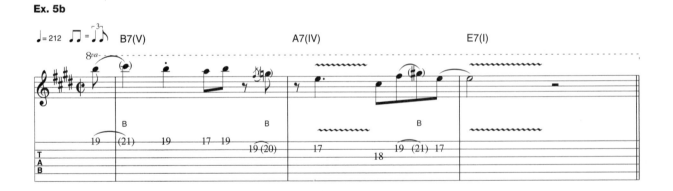

Albert King's hard-edged intensity haunts the breakdown sections of both of Zeppelin's takes on Otis Rush's rendition of Willie Dixon's "I Can't Quit You Baby" (2:48 on the *Led Zeppelin* version; 2:59 on the *Coda* take). Note the whole-step, index-finger bend in Ex. 6—remember, southpaw Albert used a flipped-over right-hand guitar and pulled the high *E* down toward the floor. Page also quotes Freddie King's famous "Hideaway" break (Ex. 7) at 9:35 into the "Whole Lotta Love" jam.

For their version of "I Can't Quit You Baby," Zeppelin emulates the Otis Rush Blues Band's 1966 Vanguard version on *Chicago/The Blues/Today*, which contains the turnaround licks absent from the original '50s Cobra release. Jimmy paraphrased many of the fills between vocals (Ex. 8a) and played the beginning of Otis's solo note-for-note (Ex. 8b). Rush's heavy attack and crammed phrasing undoubtedly made a big impression on Page.

Ex. 6

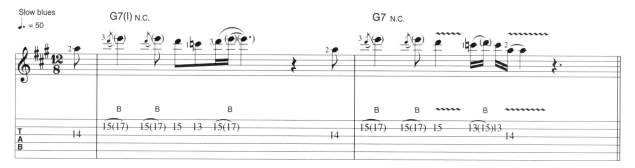

Ex. 7

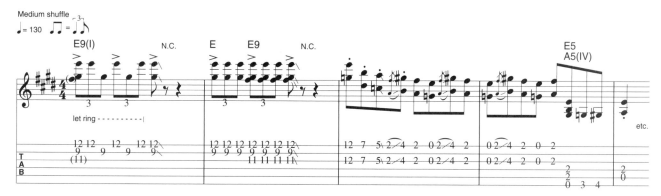

Ex. 8a

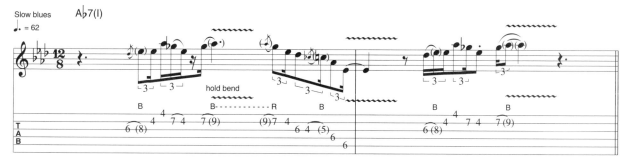

Ex. 8b

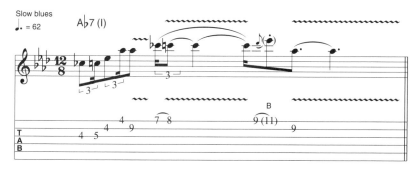

Jimmy's Delta-blues influences crop up on Zep's version of Robert Johnson's "Traveling Riverside Blues" (Ex. 9a), while Ex. 9b mixes the spooky folk stylings of sometime Page collaborator Roy Harper with the sound of the swamps. Page's unique mutations of the Delta style include "Friends," "Hats Off to Roy Harper," "Bron-Y-Aur Stomp," and "Black Country Woman," while supercharged Delta-isms abound in Zep's performances of "Celebration Day," Memphis Minnie's "When the Levee Breaks," Blind Willie Johnson's "Nobody's Fault but Mine," and the intro to "In My Time of Dying."

Ex. 9a

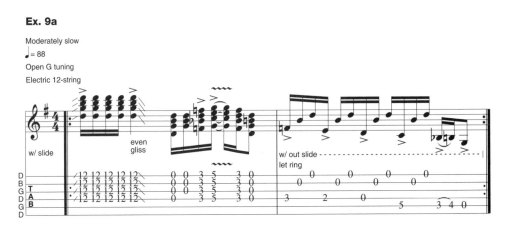

Ex. 9b

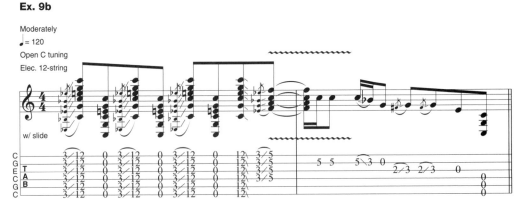

A uniquely British folk guitar style didn't really exist until after WWII. Having no indigenous guitar tradition to draw from, players like Davey Graham and Bert Jansch perfected and popularized a distinctive "folk/baroque" acoustic style. Using Jansch's preferred *DADGAD* tuning, Jimmy turned ideas from Bert's version of "Black Water Side" (outlined in Examples 10a–10e) into showcases like the Yardbirds' "White Summer" and Zep's "Black Mountain Side"—listen to *The Best of Bert Jansch* (Shanachie) to hear how the guitarist freely combines such themes. Page's other folk influences include Joni Mitchell (Zep covered "Woodstock" live), Joan Baez, Bob Dylan, and the Byrds.

Ex. 10a

Ex. 10b

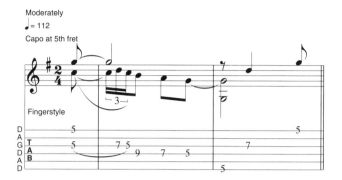

Ex. 10c

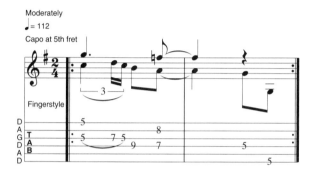

Ex. 10d

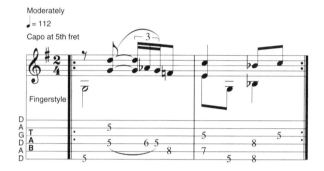

Ex. 10e

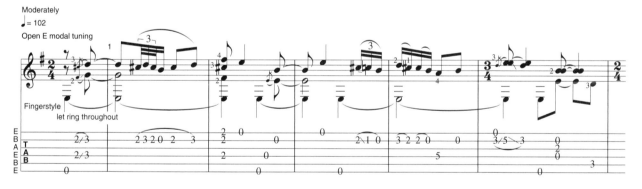

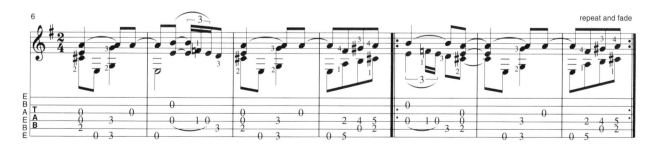

Led Zeppelin were closet funkateers. Page's James Brown/Jimmy Nolen roots emerged in the "Whole Lotta Love" jams as scratchy, syncopated dominant chords sliding in and out of the tonic by half-steps (Ex. 11a). The band would race through the verse, chorus, and solo section of "Communication Breakdown" to burst into a funky, half-time 16th-note vamp (Ex. 11b) that would often last longer than the song itself. Other Zep funk-inspired outings include "The Crunge," "Royal Orleans," "Houses of the Holy," and even "The Immigrant Song."

Ex. 11a

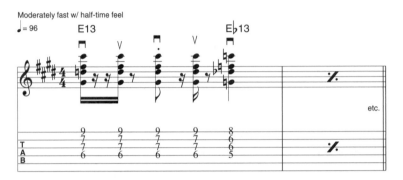

Ex. 11b

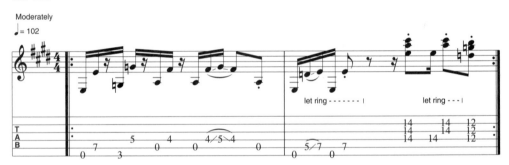

We barely have room to mention Page's country and jazz influences. Chuck Berry-style lap and pedal steel and Jimmy's sly *B*-bender licks are prominent in "Your Time Is Gonna Come," "Tangerine," "Down by the Seaside," and "Hot Dog." And consider how many guitarists probably learned their first 13th chord from "What Is and What Should Never Be" or "The Rain Song" rather than a Kenny Burrell or Wes Montgomery record.

From the Yardbirds to today, the common thread among the many facets of Jimmy Page—composer, producer, player, and sonic visionary—is not a thread at all, but a steel string.

EDDIFY ME

How Edward Van Halen Rewrote the Rock Guitar Rule Book

BY JESSE GRESS

You can't escape Eddie Van Halen's contributions to the collective guitar consciousness. From the top of the charts to movie and TV music to local guitar shop "spoo" (see *The Real Frank Zappa Book* for an explanation of this term), you'll find ample evidence of Edward's indelible mark. To the legions weaned on his playing, it's a given that Van Halen wrote the book on contemporary hard-rock guitar. But those who cut their teeth on late '60s and early '70s rock are also in Eddie's debt; he redefined the mechanics of heavy guitar just when screamin' solos had become a lost, even scorned, art. When Van Halen hit the scene, the tables turned almost overnight. It was more than okay to play hot, wild guitar on virtually any gig; it was expected. Eddie made it safe to play again!

Examples 1a through 1d are characteristic of Van Halen's "beyond blues" approach to pentatonic- and blues-scale material. Squawky pick harmonics and descending chromatic passing tones enhance the short *A* pentatonic-major fill in Ex. 1a. Example 1b begins with a syncopated, three-against-four motive derived from the 17th-position *A* pentatonic-minor scale. The 2nd (*F♯*) and 6th (*C♯*) lend Ex. 1c a Dorian vibe, while Ex. 1d blends *B* blues and Dorian elements.

Ex. 1a

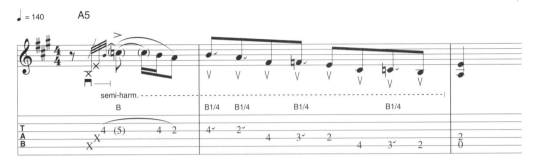

Ex. 1b

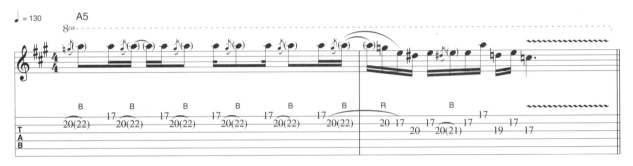

Ex. 1c

Ex. 1d

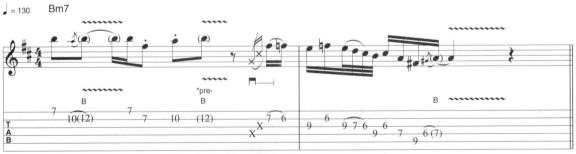

*pre-bend from 10th fret.

Many of Edward's solos climax with a precise, tremolo-picked single-string ascent followed by a high bend; the version shown in Ex. 2a is played over the IV chord (*A* in the key of *E*). The variation in Ex. 2b approaches the final bend with a short, repeated melodic sequence.

Ex. 2a

Ex. 2b

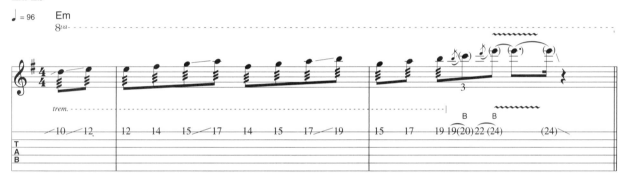

One of the most important whammy-bar innovators since Hendrix, Eddie makes frequent use of "bar-as-pick" articulations. In Ex. 3a, for example, a single pick attack accommodates the entire ascending *A* pentatonic-minor lick. Bar articulations combine with hammer-ons and pull-offs for the Mixolydian riff in Ex. 3b. The 17th-position *A* pentatonic-minor lick in Ex. 3c shifts mid-measure to a three-against-four "bar-picked" pattern with hammer-ons and pull-offs.

Ex. 3a

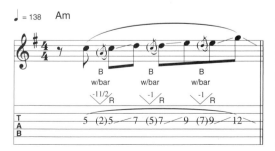

Ex. 3b

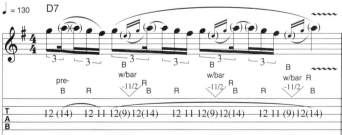

Ex. 3c

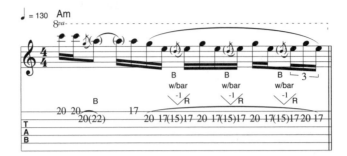

Perhaps the earliest tapping technique to catch on widely was to add notes above a bend held by the fretting hand. Example 4 illustrates a blend of bending, tapping, releasing, and pulling off. In Ex. 5a the bent note becomes a pedal tone beneath a tapped melody that outlines an *F♯* minor melodic sequence. The pedal-tone taps in Ex. 5b use descending chromatic tones for a quick, bluesy cadence; the final tonic is tapped one fret lower to compensate for the half-step bend. In Ex. 5c, the fret hand pedals two notes while the taps do the walkin'.

Ex. 4

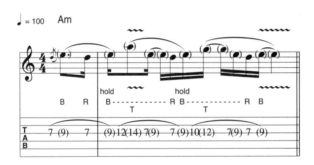

Ex. 5a

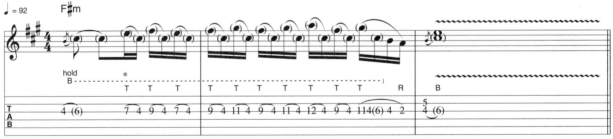

* Taps and pull-offs written at actual fretboard positions while bend is held (this example only).

Ex. 5b

Ex. 5c

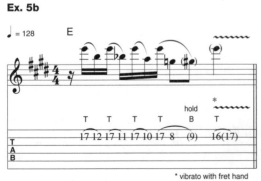

* vibrato with fret hand

Many of Edward's tapped figures are based on symmetrical fingerboard patterns. The three-against-four motive in Ex. 6a makes the *A* pentatonic riff sound more complex than it actually is. Example 6b features five-note groups with symmetrical fingerings; note Eddie's string-switching technique and syncopated, bluesy cadence. Example 7 begins with symmetrical taps and then introduces tapped slides. Try rhythmically displacing this lick by a 16th-note in either direction.

Ex. 6a

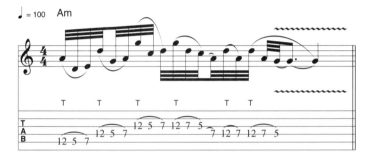

Ex. 6b

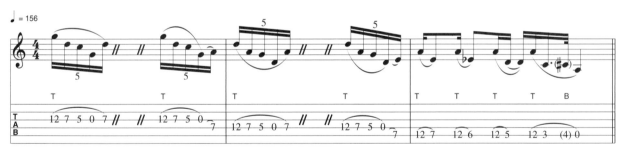

Ex. 7

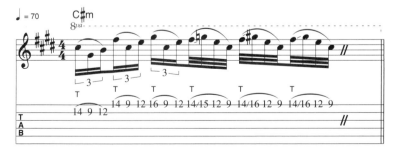

Devilishly fast tapped slides zip off the fingerboard in Ex. 8. To play the piano-style taps in Ex. 9, place your fretting hand over the top of the fingerboard and tap with your middle (m) and index (i) fingers while muting the strings toward the nut with your pinky. The picking hand, also using the middle and index fingers, taps symmetrical shapes until the last bar. The riff outlines *A7*, *B7*, *C7*, *D7*, and *E7*. Shift back to a conventional fretting-hand grip for the percussive Ex. 10. First learn the picking-hand tapping pattern—between the thumb (p) and index finger (i)—and then add the muted fretting-hand taps. This thumb/slap action is rooted in funk bass. Start slowly, gradually working it up to tempo.

Ex. 8

Ex. 9

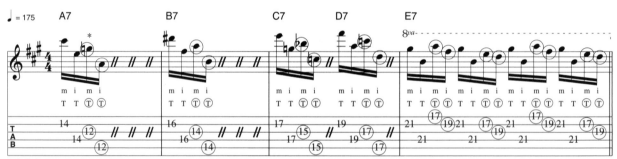

* Circled notes tapped with pick hand.

Ex. 10

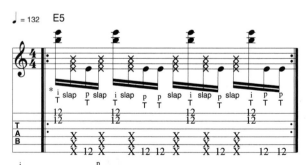

* T = tap w/ index finger, T = tap w/ thumb. Slap muted lower strings with fretting hand.

Van Halen's faux-tapping has fooled the best of 'em. Example 11 features conventional picking, but its wide fretting-hand stretches and symmetrical shapes simulate a tapped sound. Eddie also uses cross-picking with unexpected open-string punctuation for a "phantom tap" effect.

Ex. 11

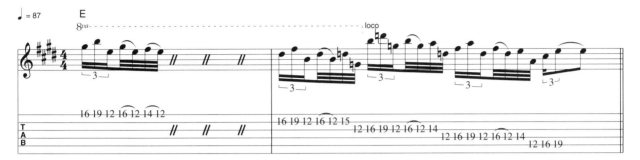

Example 12a, an angular riff based on a repeated five-note motive, contains a surprise open *E*. Try this shape accented in groups of both four and five, as well as in different fretboard positions. The fast triplets in Ex. 12b are easier than they look. Try phrasing the example in rhythmic units of four, and experiment with rhythmic displacement. Example 12c is a typically inventive Van Halen ear-catcher: A simple 5th-position *A* pentatonic-minor scale gets the cross-picked/open-string treatment. Try this one phrased in fours as well. Example 12d recalls the fretboard gymnastics of one of Eddie's heroes, Allan Holdsworth.

Ex. 12a

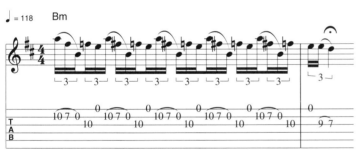

Ex. 12b

Ex. 12c

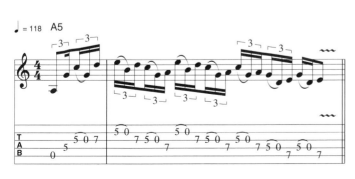

Ex. 12d

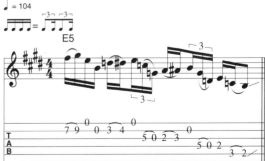

With its Beck-styled "string zips," Ex. 13 is literally all over the neck. Examples 14a through 14d showcase Edward's creative melodic and rhythmic use of natural harmonics. These licks suggest *E* minor, but they also work over other chords built from the harmonized *E* minor/*G* major scale (*F#m♭5, G, Am, Bm, C,* and *D*).

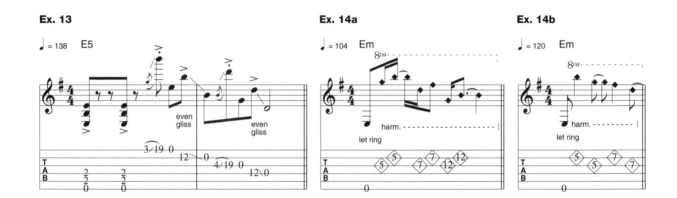

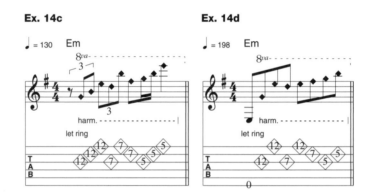

Example 15a is a virtual tapped-harmonics primer. To sound the harmonics, finger the *Asus2* chord and use short, sharp tap attacks (think "finger mallet") directly on the fret wire, 12 frets above each open or fretted note. The melody in Ex. 15b is built from chord shapes; finger each one and tap out the melody 12 frets higher. The tapped chordal harmonics in Ex. 15c are a fleshed-out variation of Ex. 15b. For tapped-harmonic chords, switch from tapping with your fingertips to the underside of your index finger. Angle your finger to approximate the diagonal shape of the *A* and *B* chords. Sympathetic notes held with the fretting hand will bleed through randomly.

Ex. 15a

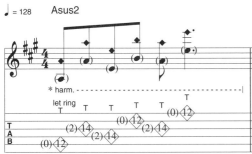

* Finger parenthesized notes and tap directly over fret 12 frets higher.

Ex. 15b

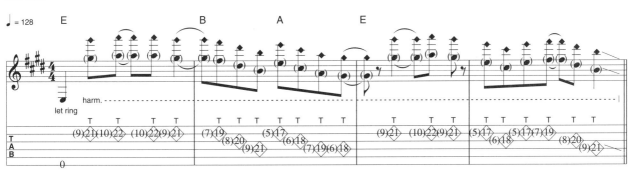

Ex. 15c

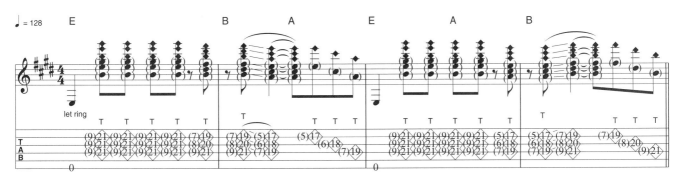

WYLDE AT HEART

Unleash Your Inner Guitar Hero with Zakk Wylde's Show-Stopping Riffs

BY JUDE GOLD

I f the phrase "less is more" were a can of beer, Zakk Wylde would crack it open against his skull, guzzle the contents, and then crush the empty with one hand. Next, staring at the crowd like a caged lion, he would launch into a cadenza of blistering blues licks, lightning-fast single-note runs, apocalyptic diminished flurries, and bone-crushing detuned passages—all delivered through walls of Marshall full-stacks so huge they're probably visible from space. Wylde is a maximalist to the core, and every time the larger-than-life guitarist steps onstage, he proves conclusively that more is, in fact, still more.

Asked what it takes to rock tens of thousands of screaming metalheads, Wylde replies, "You gotta go out there and beat some ass." And, twice a day, that's exactly what he does at Ozzfest. First he'll play a rowdy set fronting his own band, Black Label Society. Later, when darkness falls, he'll deliver his explosive guitar heroics with Ozzy Osbourne.

Despite his over-the-top onstage persona, Wylde is an inspiring player who has forged a unique, high-octane brand of lead guitar from metal, blues, classical, and even chicken pickin'. His tremendous dedication to practicing has yielded amazing dividends. Let's pretend the wild guitarist from New Jersey has just invited you onto his tour bus and handed you a gorgeous '58 Les Paul reissue and a cold brew. Now, get ready to explore his fiery riffs.

"A lot of what I play is based on pentatonic scales," explains Wylde, as he uses standard fingering to fret the *B* minor pentatonic scale in Ex. 1. The fireworks begin in Ex. 2, where Wylde applies a repeating six-note pattern to the scale using alternating pick strokes. Once you get the moves down, try playing the 16th-notes as sextuplets—six notes per downbeat. If you've noticed there is no tempo marking, that's simply because Wylde—as he does with almost all of the examples in this lesson—plays this pattern as fast as is humanly possible.

"To get fast on guitar you just have to play everything a million times. It's a matter of repetition and practice. If you don't use it, you'll lose it.

"Sometimes burning through scales sounds too mechanical—like finger exercises. That's why I have always loved bluesy rock players like Frank Marino and Robin Trower. To me, blues stuff sounds more like music."

Ex. 1   **Ex. 2**

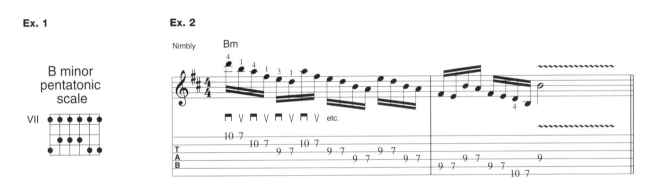

To illustrate, Wylde shifts the pentatonic box up to *E* minor and plays Ex. 3—one of his favorite phrases. The blue tinge comes from the ♭5 (*B*♭), which makes several appearances in this lick. Use your 4th finger only to fret the highest note, *A*. To get this example up to speed, try looping it, as Wylde does when he's practicing. (Notice that the last four pitches are identical to the first four, which makes bar 2's beat *four* a great place to restart the phrase.)

Ex. 3

Wylde demonstrates an even more astounding blues-inflected lick in Ex. 4, which gains an edgy chromaticism from both the major 3 (*G#*) and the juicy, sliding tritone (bar 2, "and" of beat *one*). Played fast or slow, this tasty lead is sonic gravy for the ears.

Ex. 4

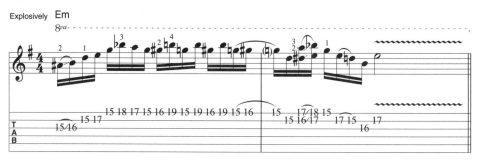

When Wylde is moving his extra-heavy Dunlop Tortex pick at full throttle, a humming-bird's wings seem slow by comparison. But when you hear those blazing riffs pouring out of Wylde's signature Marshall heads, remember the guitarist sometimes employs a trick more common to Nashville pickers than balls-to-the-wall metal mongers.

"I often throw in notes plucked by my picking hand's middle finger," Wylde reveals, playing Ex. 5 while slightly dampening the strings with the heel of his picking hand. "It's a chicken-pickin' thing that allows you to skip strings without sacrificing speed. Here, I'm flatpicking the open 5th string, hammering with my 2nd finger, and plucking the open 4th string with my middle finger. It's a repeating pattern. You can also include fretted notes on the 4th string [plays Ex. 6]; or start with a plucked note and then pull off [plays Ex. 7]."

Ex. 5

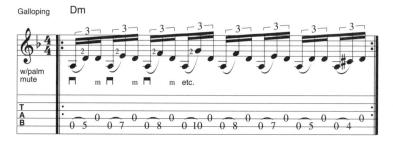

Ex. 6

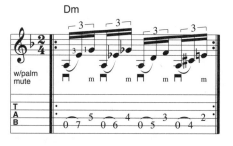

Ex. 7

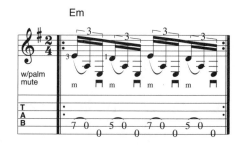

Things get even more exciting in Ex. 8, where Wylde switches to straight 16ths. This head-turning riff covers three strings and sounds like a true knuckle-buster, but it's actually easy to play. It's characteristic of Wylde's steel-string playing, which you can hear in solo acoustic pieces on Black Label Society's *1919 Eternal* and *Sonic Brew*.

Ex. 8

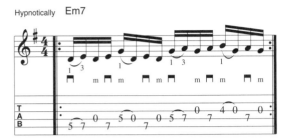

To practice Wylde's picking/plucking attack, try looping the classical motif Wylde plays in Ex. 9. In this phrase—inspired by the Isaac Albéniz composition "Leyenda"—every other note is a plucked, open *B* string. These open notes function as upper pedal tones against the descending *B* Phrygian line.

"I like to try flamenco-sounding ideas, as well," says Wylde, playing Ex. 10. In the key of *D* minor, this triplet pattern includes several middle-finger plucks.

Ex. 9

Ex. 10

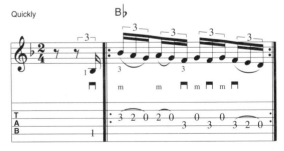

"I loved Randy Rhoads," says Wylde of his legendary predecessor in the Osbourne guitar chair. "Anybody from my generation and in my genre who says they don't is full of it. But having blond hair and a Les Paul, and being heavily influenced by classical music, I didn't want to be seen as a Randy clone. Ozzy told me, 'Just be yourself.' But that's hard to do when you don't know who you are. Then I saw an Albert Lee video."

Lee's snappy twang and mind-boggling hybrid picking inspired Wylde to inject those sounds into his hard-rocking solos. In Ex. 11, Wylde plays a vicious blues move in which, once again, he uses his picking hand's middle finger to eliminate string skips. The double-stops in bar 2 are plucked with the middle and ring (a) fingers.

"I do play finger-taps," admits Wylde, "but that's mostly when I'm playing stuff that Randy wrote for solos like 'Crazy Train' and 'Flying High Again.'"

Ex. 11

Interestingly, one of Wylde's bluesiest—and slowest—phrases is the two-handed *E* minor pentatonic bender in Ex. 12. He begins with a whole-step pre-bend on the 3rd string at the 14th fret, which he slowly releases, pulling off to the 12th fret. Next, he taps at the 21st fret with the picking hand middle finger, gradually bending this note up a whole-step before pulling it off to a pre-bent *B* that slowly drops to *A*.

"I don't use many crazy tunings," explains Wylde, "because I don't want to drastically alter the way the scales run on the fretboard. Most often, I simply lower my 6th string to *D* or *B*."

When dropping the low string a perfect 4th to *B*, Wylde uses an ultra-heavy .070 from one of his GHS signature series sets. With a string this fat, low power chords sound utterly brutal. Even if you don't detune your guitar to play the *B5* in Ex. 13, be sure to test-drive Wylde's chunky strumming pattern. This is one instance where he doesn't use alternating pick strokes, opting instead for a meaty down-up-down-down picking sequence.

Ex. 12

Ex. 13

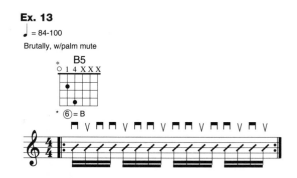

"It's about seven minutes long," says Wylde, describing the length of the extended guitar cadenza he takes during every Osbourne set. "Ozzy and the rest of the band take a break. I start off with my wah and RotoVibe pedals and take it from there. It's mostly simple stuff, but it sounds great. A lot of it is repeating licks, like this [plays Ex. 14]. Then I might go into some diminished stuff [plays Ex. 15], moving up one string at a time. When I get to the highest pair of strings, I alternate back and forth between the two [plays Ex. 16]. I like that random sound—it almost sounds computer generated."

Ex. 14

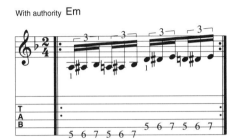

Ex. 15

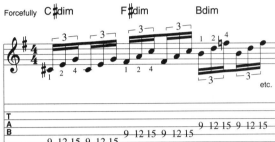

Ex. 16

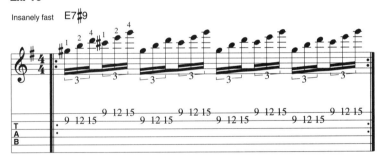

Example 17 is our final fast-and-furious Wylde pattern. Thanks to a 3rd-finger hammer and pull, this feisty repeater is easy on the picking hand. For a hypnotic effect, at the beginning of each new measure lower this lick one fret. Just remember: Like all the examples in this lesson, what this riff requires most is not chops, but conviction. "You have to play with muscle, passion, and a huge set of balls. I'll always love listening to great guitarists. Great players and great playing will never go out of style."

Ex. 17

SCARY MONSTERS

Taming the Techniques of David Bowie's Axmen

BY JAMES ROTONDI
& JOE GORE

Like Miles Davis and Frank Zappa, David Bowie has a history of hiring superb guitarists to color and drive his compositions. From Mick Ronson to Adrian Belew to Reeves Gabrels, Bowie's had an eye and ear for those who combine an experimental streak with rock 'n' roll passion and a great sense of personal style.

For all the great players he's worked with, Bowie's no slouch on the instrument himself. Famous for hard-strummed acoustic power chords like the breakdown in Ex. 1a, he also performed surprisingly supple leads during his Space Oddity period, like the one in Ex. 1b, which shows a flair for playing changes possibly inherited from his training on saxophone.

Bowie's friend Marc Bolan—whose glam-rock outfit T. Rex was a huge influence on Bowie's theatrics and groove—shared producer Tony Visconti and also shared some of his idiosyncratic lead playing on early Bowie cuts like "The Prettiest Star" and "London Bye Ta-Ta." Check out Ex. 2 to grok Bolan's style: Using only five notes, he crafts a soulful, inventive interlude with a wide, strangled vibrato and raunchy double-coil tone.

Ex. 1a

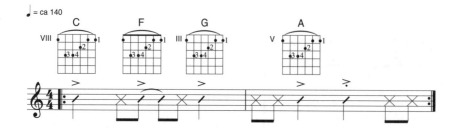

Ex. 1b

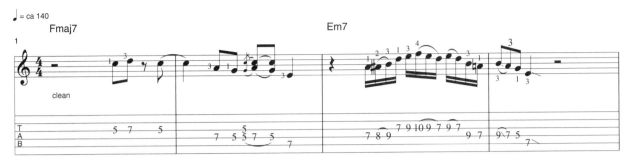

Ex. 2

Possibly the guitarist most associated with Bowie, the late Mick Ronson played on several of Bowie's seminal albums—*The Man Who Sold the World, Hunky Dory, The Rise and Fall of Ziggy Stardust and the Spiders from Mars, Aladdin Sane,* and *Pin-Ups.* A dynamite Les Paul-devoted rhythm guitarist and ahead-of-his-time texturalist, Ronson—who also worked with Bob Dylan, Lou Reed, and Morrissey—parted ways with Bowie following the recording of *Pin-Ups* in late 1973, although years later Bowie would guest on Ronson's solo LP *Heaven and Hull.*

A master of setting up songs with a burly riff, Ronson in the Ziggy Stardust era rocked big open chords like those in Ex. 3a, for which he'd often layer one just-breaking-up guitar track over one with a fixed-position wah setting for mid-boost—a main ingredient of Ronson's tough, nasal tone. Taking a stylistic cue from Jeff Beck's Yardbirds-era work, Mick also played

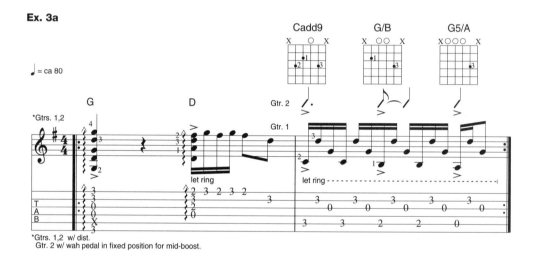

edgy, melodic leads like the two-guitar solo in Ex. 3b, which, harmonized in 3rds, recalls his playing in the very T. Rexy "Black Country Rock," available on Rykodisc's *David Bowie: Sound and Vision* box set. Of course, the beglittered Ronson had no problem pushing the envelope either, as the pentatonic-and-beyond solo in Ex. 3c—akin to Ronson's "Jean Genie" blow—amply illustrates. But signature riffs like the one in Ex. 4, often played by Bowie himself, were the real glue in any great Bowie tune, like this "Rebel Rebel"–style open-string lick, played with gusto and a cranking tube-amp tone.

By the time he joined Bowie for 1974's *Young Americans*—featuring the funk-pop smash "Fame"—rhythm ace Carlos Alomar already had a mighty impressive pedigree, having toured and recorded with James Brown, Ben E. King, Wilson Pickett, and Chuck Berry. He'd spend the next ten years working as Bowie's right-hand man and arranger on albums like *Low*, *Lodger*, *Heroes*, *Stage*, *Scary Monsters*, *Tonight*, and *Never Let Me Down*. Working with lead players such as Earl Slick, Robert Fripp, and Adrian Belew, Alomar retained his autonomy and crisp rhythm tone. "I don't usually like to play lead," he said in '87, "but when I do, I

Ex. 3c

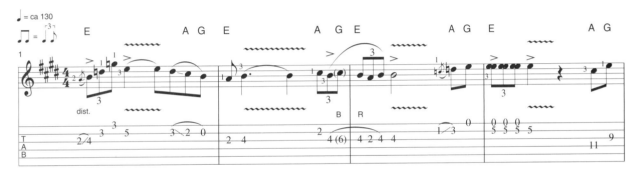

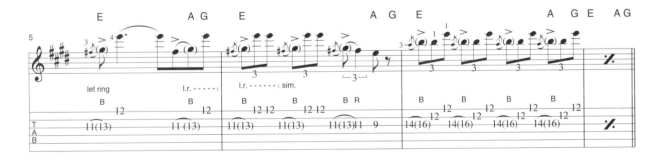

Ex. 4

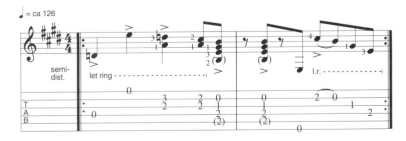

Ex. 5

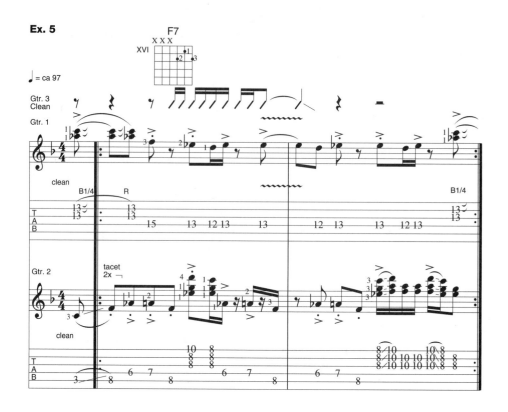

Ex. 6

like to be able to play anything I want, so when you hear me do things that sound like Earl Slick or the guitarists on old Bowie albums, it's just me taking from the other schools of playing and bringing it in." During the *Young Americans* era, Alomar was often paired with New York session cat Earl Slick, who'd go on to play on John Lennon's *Double Fantasy* and Yoko Ono's *Season of Glass*. Bringing a gritty, post-Stones style to Bowie's increasingly sophisticated sound, Slick joined the fold in 1974, when, he explained, "there was nothing that could have been bigger than playing with Bowie. David was hot then."

Alomar and Slick joined forces with Lennon on the Lennon/Bowie composition "Fame," a deliriously funky vamp with three interlocking guitars, much like the syncopated figures in Ex. 5. Guitar 1 plays single-note slurs and double-stops in the high register. Guitar 2 alternates between guttural bass notes and sweet 9s. The third guitar comps a 16th-position *F7* triad. Alomar excelled at polychordal rhythm figures like the one in Ex. 6, which recalls his phase-shifted filigrees in songs like "Golden Years"—the perky hammer-on licks also echo Clapton's funky figure on Cream's "Outside Woman Blues."

The 1979 album *Lodger* saw former Zappa and Talking Heads sideman and future King Crimsonian Adrian Belew climbing aboard and contributing tweaked whammy-bar pulsars and cool harmonic lines like those in Ex. 7a. Possibly spliced together by über-producer Brian Eno, this Belew excursion features howling tapped bends and releases coupled with growling bar dips and returns. Typical of Adrian's adventurous playing throughout *Lodger*, Ex. 7b puts a chromatic spin on an off-kilter blues lick.

Ex. 7a

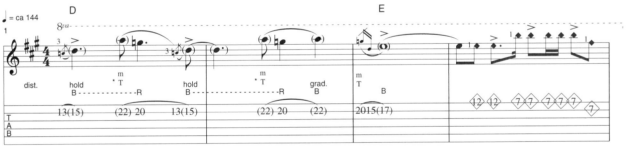

* Tap at 20th fret.

Ex. 7b

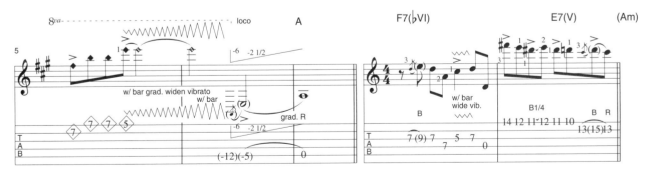

Belew's future partner in King Crimson, Robert Fripp, contributed to the Eno-produced *Heroes* in 1978 as well as 1980's *Scary Monsters*. Example 8 features the wide intervals and strange harmonies that characterized Fripp's work throughout *Scary Monsters*. After a wide-interval funk line in bar 1, the fuzzed-out tremolo-picked chords in bars 2 and 4 allude to *G7#9* and *F7#9*, with scary #9 intervals that scream "Fripp!"

By the time Bowie released *Let's Dance* in 1983, he'd installed a new guitar regime, including Chic svengali/funk powerhouse Nile Rodgers and rising Texas blues-rocker Stevie Ray Vaughan, whom Bowie had met after Vaughan's performance at the 1982 Montreux Jazz Festival. The Chic-style muted double-stops in Ex. 9a are similar to the kind of accompaniment Rodgers gave Vaughan, who'd respond with aching Albert King-style licks like those in Ex. 9b.

Ex. 8

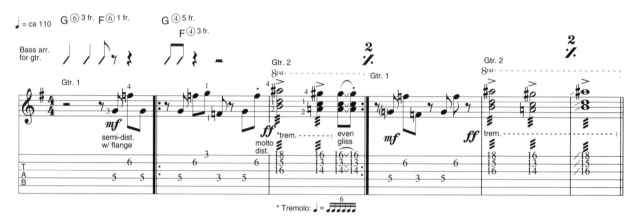

Ex. 9a

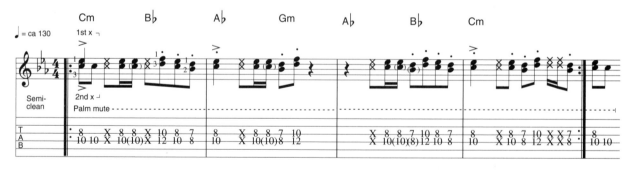

Ex. 9b

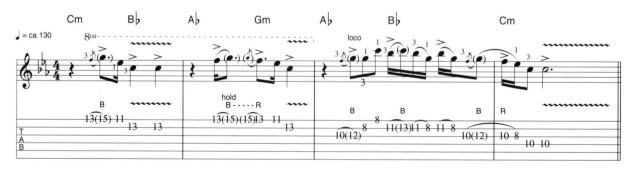

Yet another guitar shift occurred when Bowie formed Tin Machine in 1989, enlisting the talents of Reeves Gabrels, who quickly established his unique, post-shred voice with the kind of Yardbirdsy rave-up in Ex. 10a, articulated with tricky whammy embellishments and a cool hammer-on/pull-off figure. Gabrels's fleet phrasing and penchant for outside harmonies reaches its apex on Bowie's 1997 *Earthling*, which is full of stunning runs like the one in Ex. 10b. The raga-like diminished solo—a modern update of Paul McCartney's single-string solo on "Taxman"—begins with speedy tremolo picking before switching to legato in bar 3.

These certainly aren't the only guitarists to have played with Bowie. Among other star-men were Ricky Gardener (*Low*), John Hutchinson (Bowie's early demos), Chuck Hammer (the guitar synth lines on "Ashes to Ashes"), Derek Bramble (he ripped a hole in "Blue Jean"), producer Tony Visconti, and, for a single tour, the one and only Peter Frampton. Scary monsters, indeed, and not a supercreep among them.

Ex. 10a

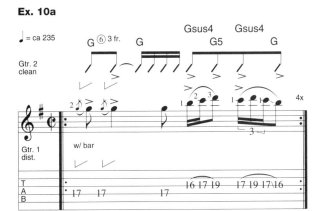
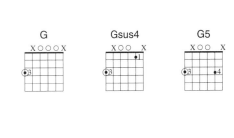

Ex. 10b

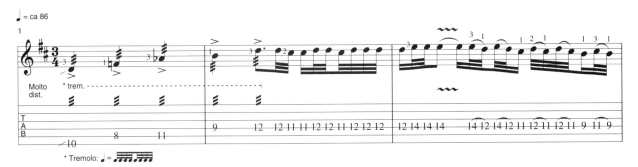

CLANG!

Players & Producers Reveal the Secrets of Heavy Tone

BY THE *GUITAR PLAYER* STAFF

DISTORTION DIARY

I like amp gain. I love the sound of speakers being tried, of tubes being beaten up. When I first started out, I got an MXR Distortion+ and said, "All right! I can do Ramones songs!" But it didn't really sound like cool Ramones guitar, just some little fuzzy thing that apologized for my lack of ability. A lot of distortion boxes compress the signal, squeezing away the tone spectrum. In general, compression turns me away.
                                        —*Kim Thayil, Soundgarden*

Distortion is kind of a lost art—a lot of kids grow up on presets and never venture beyond that. My philosophy has always been a clean amp with a stompbox. I hate the sound of piling distortion on top of distortion. Even when I'm using tube preamps, one stage will be clean and another distorted. And let's face it—there's just something about that simple, raw, gritty fuzzbox sound.

                                        —*Kirk Hammett, Metallica*

With all the processors available today, it's easy to rip through the presets and find cool tones, or use the numerous parameter controls to bring the sounds you hear in your head to life.

                                        —*K.K. Downing, Judas Priest*

If you're looking for the ultimate crunch sound, try putting a compressor after your distortion effect.

                                        —*Skunk Baxter*

When you have racks of stuff, it's an invitation to a meltdown—and there's never a quick answer if something goes wrong. With a stompbox the problem is either going to be a battery or a cable.

                                        —*Brad Whitford, Aerosmith*

I've never used any gadgets. Nothing scientific—I just turn all the dials all the way up. My only effect is a pedal without a battery that I use as an on/off switch for changing guitars.

—*Johnny Ramone*

If you lay down a huge drum kit, throbbing bass, and cranking rhythm guitar, and then try to add more guitar, those little distortion boxes don't do a hell of a lot, because they're not as complex as an amplifier in its various stages of overdrive. I find I get the best sounds by going straight into the amp, getting the mic placement and combinations just perfect, and adding the right amount of limiting or compression if I need it.

—*Joe Satriani*

I've always found that a really good distortion needs to come from two different places. You want some distortion and some clarity at the same time where you need it, so I'd set up a Fender Twin and maybe slave a little Fender Champ. I'd put [the signal] through the two amps and overload one of them—the Champ or a little Silvertone, or a Kay thing. Bump that one up, use the other one for clear, and then you can mix the two in where you want them. It's very rare on a track that you want the same sort of distortion all the way through. I like to be able to play with it, put them on separate tracks so I can juice the distortion where I want it after I've played it, because when you're playing it, you're not going to hear exactly what's going down on the tape.

—*Keith Richards*

> **We always try to find out where the distortion comes from—we overload everything. Sometimes things sound good, sometimes they sound really crappy. We like to see what a piece will do when we slam it."**
> —Paul Barker, Ministry

If I want a clean sound I just use a nice old vintage Marshall. For an ugly dirty sound I usually use the lead channel on the new Marshalls. I always have the gain set on 20. If there was 21, I'd use that. I know it fucks with your tone, but it sounds smoother. It even feels smoother on the strings.

—*Dave Navarro, Jane's Addiction*

I try to record guitar tones exactly the way I want them to sound, so there will be less to do when I mix. When I'm recording 7-string or drop-tuned guitars, I tend to record them less dirty than you might think, because as soon as you drop-tune, you lose definition. If you go with a slightly cleaner tone and double the part, it feels more powerful than a really distorted tone.

—*David Schiffman, producer (Audioslave, Nine Inch Nails,*
Rage Against the Machine, System of a Down)

If you're using an amp that's heavily overdriven, it may sound good when you're taking a solo, but it can turn into mush out in the house, especially if you're working with keyboards and other guitar players. You lose definition in the mids—in the 2kHz to 5kHz range—if there's too much gain. So if you're having trouble getting definition, just plug straight into a cleaner amp. Then if you need a bit of juice for your solos, just tweak it with a fuzztone or some other kind of boost.

—*Joe Perry, Aerosmith*

I like to have the signal from the guitar to be not distorted. I don't like hot-output pickups, because there are so many overtones that don't get through. Also, if you play 9ths or minor chords and shit like that with amp distortion and a distorted pickup, it mushes. I use really old Marshall 50-watt heads, Mark IIs from between '68 and '72, and put the clean signal from the pickup through an additional preamp, so the signal coming out of the preamp is very clean, but it's loud. The Marshall is the sole source of the distortion. On the amplifier I usually have the preamp's gain very, very high, and its output somewhere between half and three-quarters. I like a distorted sound where a single note doesn't sound distorted—it just sounds sweet—so unless you play a 5th power chord, it shouldn't sound distorted. That's my trick.

—*Yngwie Malmsteen*

POWER PLAYS

Don't play so busy! When you're taking up all the space playing a million miles per hour, it thins out the sound. But when you're playing a solid riff and the other instruments are complementing you, it's easy to make the guitar sound huge.

—*Daron Malakian, System of a Down*

A part of making guitars sound huge is psychological—it's where things sit in the mix and at what moment they get louder. People talk about the huge sound of John Bonham's drums on Led Zeppelin records, but in reality they only sound huge when nothing else is playing.

—*Rick Rubin, producer (System of a Down, Red Hot Chili Peppers, Beastie Boys)*

> **" Nothing sounds better than a great guitar coming out of a cabinet. Once you have that incredible source sound, the best you can do is try to capture it accurately."**
>
> —Kevin Shirley, producer
> (Dream Theater, Led Zeppelin,
> Iron Maiden, Jimmy Page, Joe Satriani,
> Rocket from the Crypt)

When I listen to a lot of older records like Zeppelin, the guitars aren't anywhere near as loud or wide-sounding as something on one of our records or a Tad or a Helmet record. So why do they sound so heavy? It's just the nature of the riff and of the room the mix allows for the bass to get underneath the guitar to make this nice solid wall of the two instruments.

—*Kim Thayil*

Take a Supro amp and a Tele, and you'll nick that *Led Zeppelin I* sound perfectly.

—*Chris Goss, Masters of Reality*

We like dropped tunings, but we wanted to avoid that "nu-metal" sound. So on dropped-*A* songs such as "Stop" and "March of Hope," my guitar is tuned standard except for the lowest string, where I use a bass string and tune it to low *A*. My two bottom strings are in octaves, which gives me a really heavy sound that's still clear, and my overtones don't clash with what Acey [Slade] is doing.

—*Virus, Dope*

I can't play through a small amp for an entire recording. I've got to have that big-amp impact along with the ambience of the room. There's a lot of complexity in a distorted guitar tone, and it needs some room to breathe.

—*Andy Hawkins, Blind Idiot God*

I don't use compression when tracking guitars, because usually the amp's tubes are already compressing the sound, and I don't like to spoil it. Additional compression also tends to muddy up the top end; one of the nice things about high-gain amps is that they've often got amazingly clear and beautiful top-end.

—Michael Beinhorn, producer (Korn, Marilyn Manson,
Ozzy Osbourne, Red Hot Chili Peppers, Soundgarden)

Little amps tracked as loud as they can go—that's it!

—Chad Gracey, Live

Get a Palmer Speaker Simulator. Instead of using an amp modeler or preamp, you can plug the speaker output of the amp you love straight into the Palmer and get your tone.

—Joe Barresi, producer (Melvins, Fu Manchu,
Limp Bizkit, Powerman 5000)

For a lot of parts [on the Red Hot Chili Peppers' *Blood Sugar Sex Magik*], even solos, I just went straight into the board. You can get amazing, funky tones that way. In fact, a lot of my distortion is from overdriving the board.

—John Frusciante, Red Hot Chili Peppers

My '69 Marshall is turned all the way up—everything's on 10—and the two channnels are jumped so I can get that low end out of the second channel.

—Brad Whitford, Aerosmith

[A heavy sound] has to do with how deep the groove is—it's not about playing fast or scooping the mids. All of my super-heavy riffs were tracked with single-coil pickups, so the heaviness has to come from the playing.

—Tom Morello, Rage Against the Machine

The power you get from cranking a guitar through tubes is peerless—it's something you can't get any other way.

—Eric Powell, 16 Volt

Guitarisms

I need a really high-output guitar because I'm the only guitar player in Jane's Addiction—I need to cover a lot of sonic ground. Les Pauls used to do that for me. I had to switch to Strats for the Chili Peppers because their sound is a bit thinner than Jane's Addiction. Now, with the Paul Reed Smiths, I have a high-output sound that's similar to the Les Paul, but it's not as weighty. It's a slinkier feel, and there's a little more versatility in the pickup choices.

—Dave Navarro

The key—downpicking! It's tighter-sounding and a lot chunkier.

—James Hetfield, Metallica

" I've always thought the guys with the best tone are the ones who just grab a guitar and make it sound like something solid."

—Slash

I prefer to listen to my amp rather than to monitors, so I have very little of my guitar sound coming out of the monitors. I just walk around and find the sweet spot where I can hear the amp really well.

—Joe Perry, Aerosmith

Some amazing things start to happen when you turn the guitar's volume down and the amp up. That capacitance creates all sorts of phenomenal tones.

—Chad Gracey, Live

People think they can drop-tune and scoop out the mids, but when you're tuning that low you've got to have midrange. It may sound killer when you're standing in front of an amp, but once you put a snare drum or ride cymbal on top of it the guitar disappears. What's the use of having this crushing heavy tone if you can't distinguish what it is?

—Pepper Keenan, Corrosion of Conformity

When I started playing wah, it wasn't for the actual "wah" sound, but for the variations in tone. Even now I hardly ever go *wah-wah*—I use more of a sweep, starting in the full-bass position and moving and moving to the full-treble position, emphasizing certain frequencies in certain parts of the lick.

—Kirk Hammett

Here's a cool trick: If you lower your pickups, the squealing feedback will go away and you can keep your gain [high].

—Geno Lenardo, Filter

Guitars can be finicky. There are collectible guitars—like a '52 Les Paul goldtop—that you look at and say, "That's going to be the voice of God." Then you listen to it, and it sounds like crap. But a master musician can make almost any guitar sound good. It's a really elusive combination of the instrument, the amplifier, and the player.

—Michael Beinhorn

Ninety-nine percent of great tone is in your fingers, so keep working on your technique. And don't let the guitar be the boss—dig into the guitar like you want to beat the crap out of it. When your playing is tentative, it's reflected in your tone.

—David Schiffman

I always use metal plectrums, which bring out the high harmonic squeals.

—Justin Broadrick, Godflesh

[For Metallica's *Load*] we would do anything to get an interesting sound. We did a lot of blending old stompboxes with the newest technology, like using an Eventide effect with an old Electro-Harmonix Electric Mistress pedal or some distortion pedal that was only made for six months in 1967. One thing we used consistently was an MXR Phase 100. In the past we'd always go running for some slick flanger, but the Phase 100 fit so much better than any rackmounted sound. We used a lot of Roland VG-8 [modeling system], which I found to be great when mixed with more traditional sounds. I really like the way you can mutate a VG-8 sound and then blend it with, say, some old miked amps. You can hear that on the heavily tremoloed wah part right before the guitar solo on "2x4."

—Kirk Hammett

The longest cable I use is a 20-foot Monster Cable that goes from a Samson wireless into my amps. Using as short a cable as possible between the wireless and the amp is the key to better tone.

—Joe Perry

I really love how the sound of small amps translates to tape. When you crank one up it has to work really hard—that's how you get great tone.

—Warren Haynes, Gov't Mule

The trick to creating a wall of guitars is using very little distortion on the rhythm parts.

—Mikael Akerfeldt, Opeth

MICROPHONICS

I put Shure SM57s in front of the cabinets and place an AKG C414 out in the room. Nothing records guitars better than a 57.

—Art Alexakis, Everclear

I always use a splitter to run the guitar to multiple amps, and then I blend everything down to one track. If I'm miking a 4x12 cabinet, I'll put a Shure SM57 and a Senneheiser MD-421 in close to the grille, to keep the direct signal as phase-accurate as possible.

—Joe Barresi

> **The key is one mic, one amp. No matter how you try to invert your phase or whatever, having more than one mic and one amp creates phase cancellation."**
>
> —Chad Gracey, Live

I place the mics as close to the speaker cone as possible. I don't like ambient sound, so I don't use room mics.

—Michael Beinhorn

I'm still using basically the same technique I used back in the Beatle days—which is to position a Neumann U47 wherever the guitar or amp sounds the best.

—Geoff Emerick, producer/engineer (Beatles, Jeff Beck, Cheap Trick, Mott the Hoople, Nazareth, Split Enz, Supertramp, Robin Trower, Ultravox)

I don't need eight different microphones on one speaker cabinet, and I don't like room sound on a guitar, because it washes things out.

—Nuno Bettencourt

KEEPING IT REAL

Our production philosophy is to play your guitar part with a beer in your hand, or turn the board gain up so hot that the mic picks up everything in the room. If Patrick [Leisegang] accidentally knocks something over, it could be interesting. If someone walks into the room or the telephone rings, that's all valid.

—Richard Patrick, Filter

Don't track guitars in isolation. Rehearse your material so you know what the hell you're doing when you walk in the studio, track the thing as live as possible with a band, and if you have to punch in a guitar part, don't belabor the point. After all, it's got to have some hair on it.

—Eddie Kramer, producer (Anthrax, Deep Purple,
Jimi Hendrix, Kiss, Led Zeppelin)

Spend time improving your recording techniques on your home setup, but don't ignore the basic tenet of "practice, practice, and more practice." Page, Clapton, and Hendrix didn't just pick up their instruments and immediately start playing like guitar gods.

—Shel Talmy, producer (the Creation, the Kinks, the Who)

I like to track on 2" analog tape at 15ips to capture the fattest tone, but I mix using Pro Tools. It's hard to make a record without Pro Tools these days, because the record companies want things to zing this way and that way like a video game. They're convinced that kids need the constant stimulation of things panning and changing all the time.

—Kevin Shirley

> **" I defy engineers who try to clean things up. We like noise, we like feedback, and we like noisy drums and gurgling bass lines. There just has to be depth, clarity, and integrity in the overall delivery."**
> —Ted Nugent

There are a couple of reasons I've switched to Pro Tools. The biggest is that the sound of digital has come a long way—it's not as thin sounding as it used to be. Creatively, the advantages of hard-disk recording are huge.

—Chris Goss, Masters of Reality

I always printed reverb and compression to tape, and committing to a sound while tracking stays with me to this day. Otherwise, you wind up editing in Pro Tools for months. I mean, come on guys, it's rock 'n' roll! The reason Zeppelin, Hendrix, and the Stones sound so marvelous is because there was crap on those tracks—there was dirt, hiss, noise, and mistakes. Admittedly, we're talking about great musicians, but still, listen to those records—the tempos go up and down like a bloody yo-yo, there are mistakes everywhere, and the great thing about these artists is that they would capitalize on the mistakes.

—Eddie Kramer

HEAR 'EM ALL

A Metal Discography

Nuno Bettencourt
(w/Extreme)
III Sides to Every Story,
    A&M

Ritchie Blackmore
(w/Deep Purple)
Deep Purple in Rock, EMI
Fireball, Warner Bros.
Machine Head, Warner
    Bros.
Made in Japan, Empire

Jerry Cantrell
Degradation Trip,
    Roadrunner
(w/Alice in Chains):
Dirt, Columbia

Ace Frehley
(w/Kiss)
Alive, Polygram Int'l

Marty Friedman
Music for Speeding,
    Favored Nations
Dragon's Kiss, Shrapnel
(w/Megadeth; both on
    Capitol):
Countdown to Extinction
Rust in Peace

Tony Iommi
(w/Black Sabbath; both
    on Victor)
Paranoid
Master of Reality

George Lynch
(w/Dokken; both on
    Elektra/Asylum)
Tooth and Nail
Under Lock and Key

Dave Navarro
(w/Jane's Addiction;
    both on Warner Bros.)
Nothing's Shocking
Ritual de lo Habitual

Jimmy Page
(w/Led Zeppelin; both on
    Atlantic)
Led Zeppelin
Led Zeppelin II

Randy Rhoads
(w/Ozzy Osbourne)
Blizzard of Ozz, Jet
Diary of a Madman, Jet
Tribute, Sony
(w/Quiet Riot):
The Randy Rhoads Years,
    Rhino

Pete Townshend
(w/the Who)
The Who Sell Out,
    Polygram Int'l
Live at Leeds, MCA

Eddie Van Halen
(w/Van Halen; both on
    Warner Bros.)
Van Halen
Van Halen II

Zakk Wylde
(w/Black Label Society;
    both on Spitfire)
1919 Eternal
Sonic Brew

AC/DC
(Angus & Malcolm
    Young)
Back in Black, Epic

Aerosmith
(Joe Perry, Brad Whitford)
Toys in the Attic, Sony
Rocks, Columbia

Judas Priest
(K.K. Downing,
    Glenn Tipton)
Stained Class, Columbia

Iron Maiden
(David Murray,
    Adrian Smith)
The Number of the Beast,
    Sony

Metallica
(Kirk Hammett,
    James Hetfield)
Kill 'Em All, Elektra
Ride the Lightning, DCC
Master of Puppets, Elektra
Load, Elektra

Motörhead
(Fast Eddie Clarke)
Ace of Spades, Sanctuary

Pantera
(Dimebag Darrell)
Vulgar Display of Power,
    EastWest

**Red Hot Chili
    Peppers**
(John Frusciante)
Blood Sugar Sex Magik,
    Warner Bros.

Slayer
(Kerry King,
    Jeff Hanneman)
Reign in Blood, Universal

Coal Chamber
(Meegs Rascon)
Coal Chamber, Road
    Runner

Korn
(Munky, Head)
Issues, Sony Int'l

Limp Bizkit
(Wes Borland)
*Chocolate Starfish and the
    Hotdog Flavored Water*,
    Interscope

Staind
(Mike Mushok)
Break the Cycle,
    Flip/Elektra

System of a Down
(Daron Malakian)
System of a Down, Sony

PHOTO CREDITS

WHEN IT COMES TO GUITARS, WE WROTE THE BOOK.

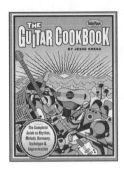

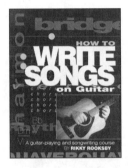
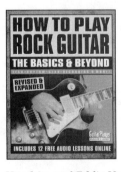
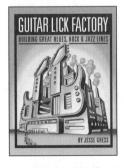